Contents

To the teacher

This book follows a slightly different format from many of the books in the 'Knowing' series because many of the chapters present pupils with historical evidence in the form of short extracts from speeches and writings, or photographs and illustrations. This evidence is used as part of the learning process but it does not dominate the book to the exclusion of all narrative. The author believes that narrative has been much undervalued in recent years and consequently the narrative in this book aims to capture the pupils' interest by tying complex historical events to everyday experiences. The pupils are often encouraged to think about the world they know and apply the lessons to the world they are learning about.

The language level is such that the book can be easily understood by pupils with a reading age of ten and over yet at the same time the adoption of a patronising tone has been avoided.

Questions

The author believes that pupils learn best when they are involved in handling historical evidence to answer questions. But pupils cannot be expected to answer questions without adequate guidance. The questions are therefore varied in nature. Their purpose is

1 to provide the basis for extended thought about the issues raised;
2 to guide the pupils in making notes on the subject;
3 to enable the pupils to examine historical evidence before reaching a decision about an answer;
4 to promote empathetic reconstruction of the past.

GCSE

This book is aimed at students in the 3rd to 5th years of secondary schools, many of whom will be studying history for the GCSE. It can be used with mixed ability or streamed groups: the reading level makes it accessible to all students and the questions are designed in such a way that differentiation between pupils can be achieved by outcome. The questions lend themselves to different levels of response in the way that the GCSE examination intends.

Superpower crisis points, 1945–86

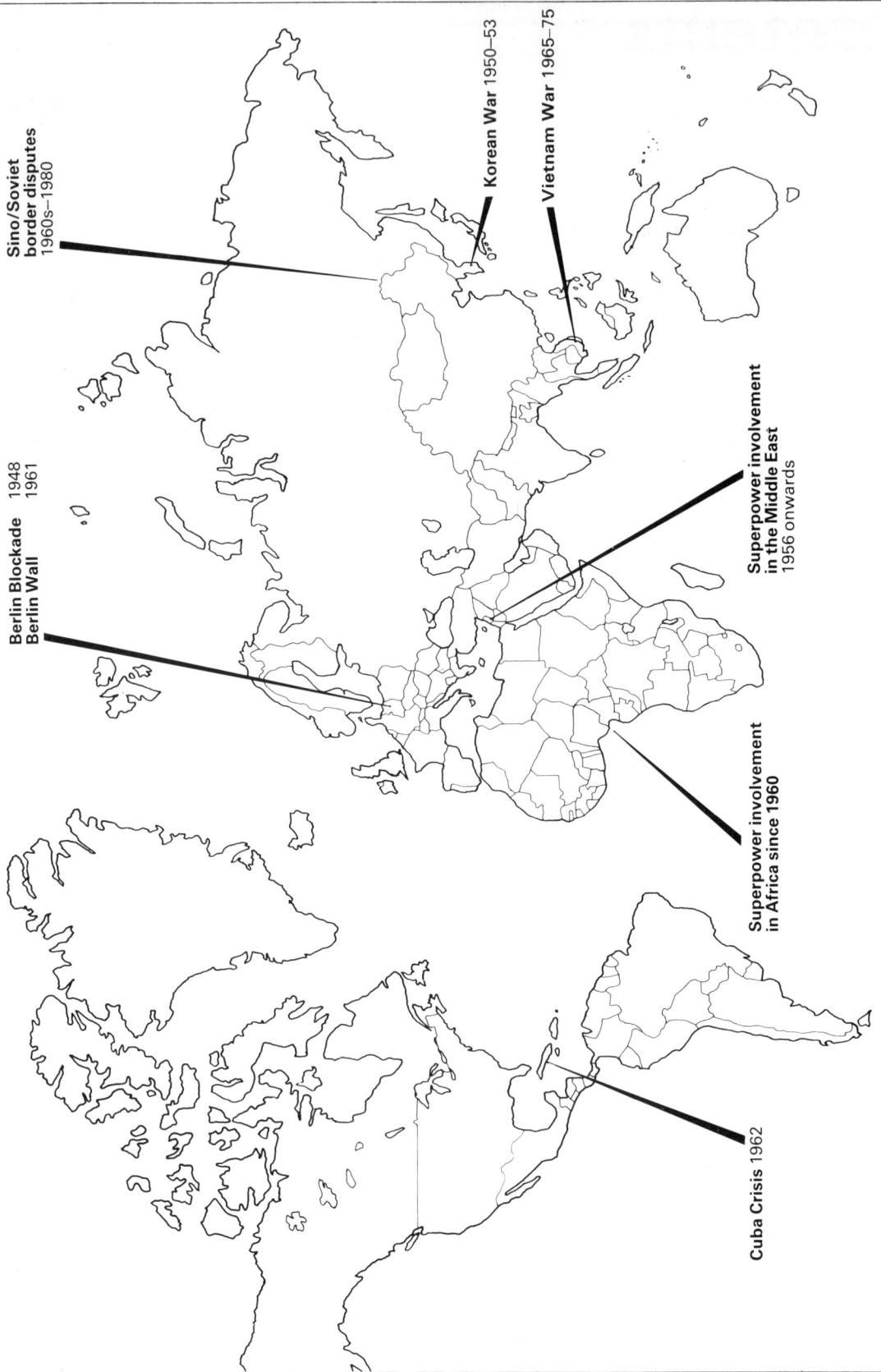

Sino/Soviet
border disputes
1960s–1980

Korean War 1950–53

Vietnam War 1965–75

Berlin Blockade   1948
Berlin Wall   1961

Superpower involvement
in the Middle East
1956 onwards

Superpower involvement
in Africa since 1960

Cuba Crisis 1962

4

S

er
ns
45
[artley

UNWIN HYMAN

ACKNOWLEDGEMENTS

The author and publisher would like to thank the following for permission to reproduce photographs in this publication.

Allsports (Tony Duff) Source A, page 38   Associated Press Ltd 9, 20, 32 (top) (Nguyen Kong), 35, 45 (Source D), 46   BBC Hulton Picture Library 14, 15, 18   Bilderdienst Süddeutscher Verlag 19   HMSO 43   John Hillelson Agency Ltd (John Pierre Laffont/Sygma) 22 (left), 26, 33 (© Ian Berry, Magnum) John Topham Picture Library 20   Novosti Press Agency 11 (left)   The Photo Source 23, 28, 37   Popperfoto 7, 17, 22 (right), 24, 25, 27, 30, 31, 39 (Source C), 45 (Sources B and C)   Rex Features Ltd 39 (Source B), 47   Three Lions (Orlando) 10, 11 (right)

We would like to acknowledge the following sources used for extracts and illustrations:

The Contemporary World by Canon, Clarke and Smuga (Oliver & Boyd) Source D, page 29 and Source B, page 34   *Daily Express* article of 9 July 1948, Source C, page 19   *Documents on World History 2* by J. Wroughton and D. Cook (Macmillan) Source D, page 33   *The Economist* article of August 1961, Source B, page 28   *Europe in the Twentieth Century* by A. L. Funk (Dorsey Press) Source D, page 19   *Guardian Weekly* 22 January 1984, Source C, page 37   *In Our Time* by Geoffrey Hodgson (Macmillan) Source E, page 33   *Latin America and the Caribbean, a Handbook,* ed. C. Velis, (A. Blond), Source A, page 30   *Modern China* by C. K. Macdonald (Basil Blackwell) Source B, page 15   'Protect and Survive' government pamphlet (HMSO), Source C, page 43   *Sunday Express* article of 1 March 1987, Source A, page 45   *Super Power Rivalry* by John Sayer (Edward Arnold) Source A, page 36   *The Twentieth Century* by John Hamer (Macmillan) Source C, page 16 and Source B, page 20   *World History from 1914 to the Present Day* (Collins) Source B, page 32   *World Powers in the Twentieth Century* by Harriet Ward (BBC/Heinemann) Source E, page 29   *World War Three, A Military Projection Founded on Today's Facts* ed. S. Biswell (Hamlyn) Source A, page 42 and Source B, page 34.

We regret that we have been unable to trace the copyright holders of Source B, page 41.

Further reading

There are many suitable school textbooks on this subject. I have found the following most useful both in my teaching and in my preparation of this book.

The Contemporary World by Cannon, Clark and Smuga (Oliver & Boyd)
Contemporary Files the World by W. P. Rae (Heinemann)
World Powers in the Twentieth Century by Harriet Ward (BBC)
Super Power Rivalry by John Sayer (Edward Arnold)
'Making History' World History 1914 to the Present Day by Christopher Culpin (Collins)
Modern Russia by L. Hartley (Bell & Hyman)

Published by
UNWIN HYMAN LIMITED
15/17 Broadwick Street
London W1V 1FP

First published in 1988 by Bell & Hyman Limited

Reprinted 1989

British Library Cataloguing in Publication Data
Hartley, Larry
Superpower relations since 1945.
(Knowing world history).
1. World politics—1945–
I. Title   II. Series
327'.09'04   D844
ISBN 0-7135-2787-0

Illustrations by Paul Allingham

Printed and bound by
Bell & Bain Ltd, Glasgow

Instructions for the 'consequences exercise' in Chapter 21

'Events' such as the following can be written on the paper to start the consequence exercise.
1 'A Russian airliner containing 300 passengers is shot down over American airspace suspected of spying'.
2 'An American airliner is shot down over Russian airspace suspected of spying. There are 300 passengers'.
3 'Chinese leaders accuse Russia of becoming too friendly with the USA'.
4 'The USA refuses to stop developing its Starwars programme'.

Alternatively the teacher can write the same event on each piece of paper and see if the groups come up with different consequences.

Time chart

1   Who are the superpowers?

The USA (United States of America), China and the USSR (Union of Soviet Socialist Republics) are often known as the *superpowers*. Have you ever wondered why this is so? Sources A and B show how much they deserve this title. These three nations are very powerful. They have enormous populations. Between them they take up nearly a third of the land space in the world. They control more than half of the world's wealth, or money, and they have massive armed forces and supplies of weapons. The map on page 4 shows the other countries that each superpower can influence.

1 Mark the following onto an outline map of the world and draw a key to show what you have done.
   a Shade in red the largest superpower in land area.
   b Shade in blue the wealthiest superpower.

c Shade in yellow the superpower with the largest population.

China is not yet as powerful as the other two superpowers. However, she has the world's largest population and if she manages to organise herself better, then she might easily become the most powerful country in the world.

2 a Which of the following things shown in Sources A and B do you think is the most important when deciding which of the superpowers is the most powerful?
      i   Wealth
      ii Land area
      iii Population
      iv Armed forces
      Explain the reason for your choice.

Source A   *Superpower strengths*

	China	USSR	USA
Population (in millions)	1000 m	250 m	220 m
Wealth (in billions of dollars, GNP)	200	600	1600
Inter continental ballistic missiles	?	1477	1054
Long-range bombers	60	135	373
Armed forces	3 960 000	4 412 000	3 860 000

Source B   *The sizes of the superpowers. If the land belonging to the three superpowers was piled up with the largest at the bottom it would look like this. (Britain is there for comparison.) The figures show the percentage of the world's surface that each superpower occupies.*

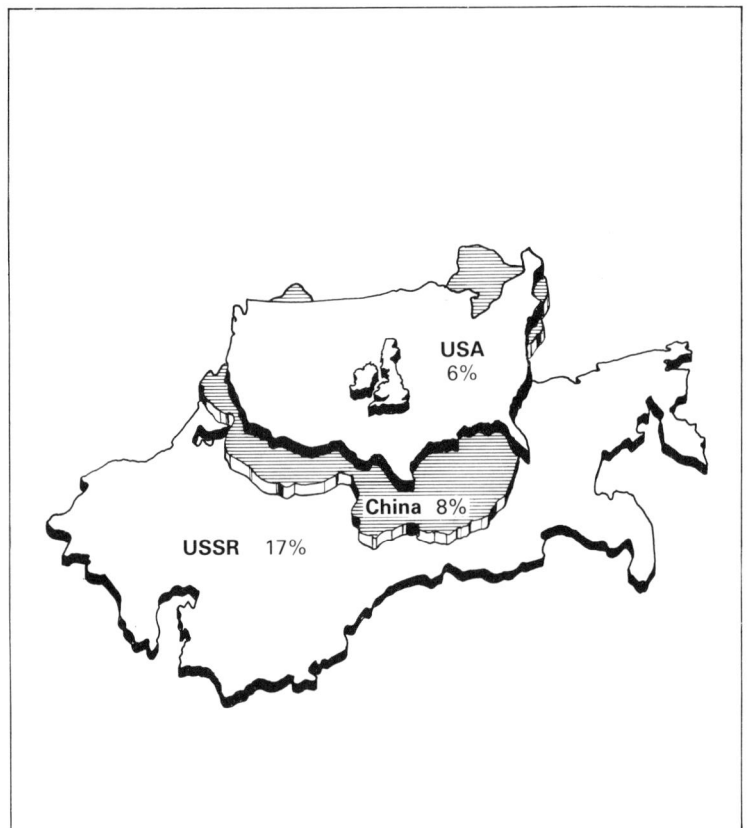

USA 6%

China 8%

USSR 17%

```
┌────────────────────────────────────────────┐
│            The Security Council              │
│              Permanent members               │
│      USA   USSR   China   France   Britain   │
│  10 other countries are elected to the council│
│             for a two year term.             │
└────────────────────────────────────────────┘
```

```
┌──────────────────────────────────────────────────────┐
│                  The General Assembly                  │
│    149 world countries send 5 representatives each.    │
│  A two-thirds majority is needed before any action is passed. │
│                                                        │
└──────────────────────────────────────────────────────┘
```

Source C *The organisation of the United Nations. The photograph shows a meeting of the Security Council*

Not everything that happens in the world is controlled by these superpowers. But they are certainly involved in most decisions.

In 1945 the United Nations Organisation was set up as a peace-keeping force. (See Source C.) All three superpowers now have seats on the Security Council. This means that they can veto (stop) any action that the UN might want to take against any of them. This makes them very powerful indeed. The UN has only been able to send troops to fight against a superpower once since 1945. This was in 1950 when they sent soldiers to stop Russian troops invading South Korea. (See Chapter 9). The Russians were not able to veto this decision because they had walked out of the Security Council meeting. They had walked out in protest against the fact that China had been given a seat on the Security Council.

Most of this book is about disputes between superpowers like the one between China and Russia (the USSR) in 1950. Most of these disputes have been between the USA and the USSR and these have become known as the Cold War. (See Chapter 2.)

3 a **What was the United Nations set up for?**
   b **What is a veto and which *five* nations can use it?**
   c **Why was the UN able to send troops into Korea in 1950?**

4 **Write out the following paragraph filling in the blanks by looking back over this chapter. Call it 'The Superpowers'.**

China, Russia and America are known as superpowers. ____ has the largest population of the three but Russia has the largest ____ ____ [two words]. ____ is the wealthiest. All three nations along with ____ and ____ have seats on the Security Council of the UN. This means that they can ____ any decisions that might be taken against them. The ____ has the largest armed forces; it has ____ men in its armies. But the ____ has more long-range bombers than either of the others. The dispute between two of these superpowers, the USA and the USSR has become known as the ____ War.

2 What is the Cold War?

Source A *The Cold War game*

Have you ever played a game of chess or draughts? (See Source A.) Or perhaps you have played a computer game where you try to score more points than your opponent. In games like these you spend a lot of time trying to work out what the other person is going to do next. Is there someone in your class or school that you do not get on with very well? You must often wonder what they are thinking or why other people seem to like them. In some ways this is what the USA and USSR are like towards each other. Source A is meant to show the leaders of these countries looking at each other across a chess board and wondering what the other one is going to do next. But the USA and USSR are not playing a game. Any moves that *they* make can affect the whole world. This is what this book is going to show you.

An American newspaper reporter said, just after the Second World War in 1946, 'We are in the midst [middle] of a *cold war*.' He meant that the USA and USSR were rivals. They both wanted power. They were both suspicious of each other. What ever one of them did, the other one saw it as a threat. It is called a *Cold War* because they never actually fight each other. They just try to make sure that they are stronger or that other people think they are better than the other side.

1 **Copy out the following sentences missing out the phrases that are wrong.**

The USA and USSR are involved in a hot war/cold war.
This means that they do/do not actually fight each other.
Each one tries to prove that the other one is stronger/weaker than they are.

2 **In what ways is the Cold War like a game of chess?**

How the Cold War has developed

Source B shows five steps in the relationship between the USA and USSR. One of these steps (1945–57) was a period of confrontation, or argument. The other four steps were the different methods that the two superpowers have used to try to avoid confrontation.

Source B *Steps in the Cold War*

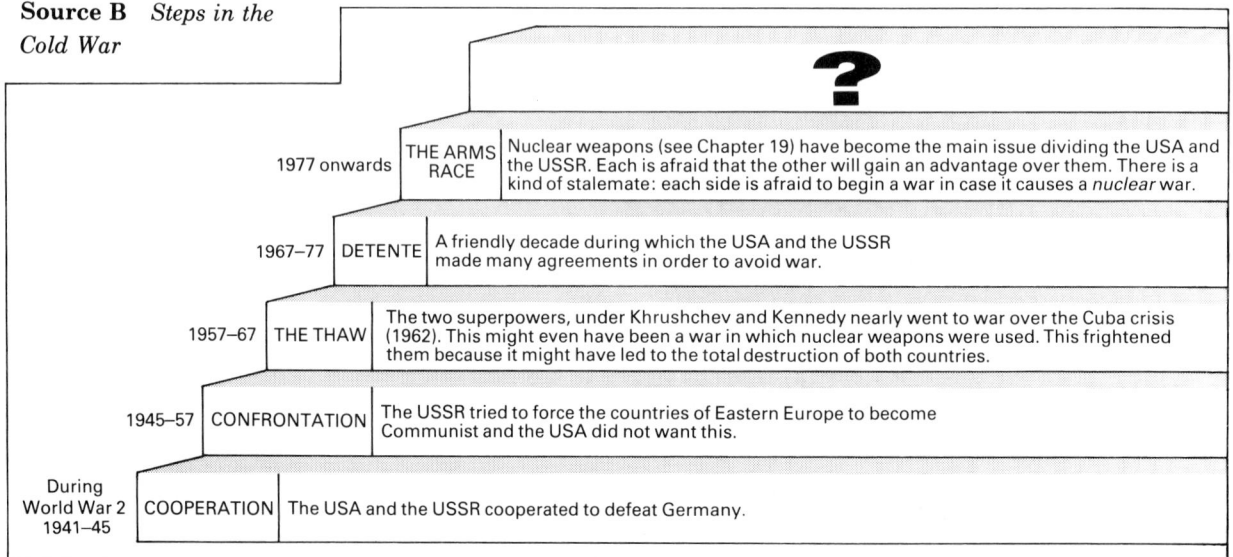

1977 onwards	THE ARMS RACE	Nuclear weapons (see Chapter 19) have become the main issue dividing the USA and the USSR. Each is afraid that the other will gain an advantage over them. There is a kind of stalemate: each side is afraid to begin a war in case it causes a *nuclear* war.
1967–77	DETENTE	A friendly decade during which the USA and the USSR made many agreements in order to avoid war.
1957–67	THE THAW	The two superpowers, under Khrushchev and Kennedy nearly went to war over the Cuba crisis (1962). This might even have been a war in which nuclear weapons were used. This frightened them because it might have led to the total destruction of both countries.
1945–57	CONFRONTATION	The USSR tried to force the countries of Eastern Europe to become Communist and the USA did not want this.
During World War 2 1941–45	COOPERATION	The USA and the USSR cooperated to defeat Germany.

3　**a**　What *are* the four methods, since 1941, that the USA and USSR have used to try to avoid going to war against each other?

　　b　Do you think the present way, 'the arms race', is more or less likely than the other four to lead to war? Explain your answer.

The USSR controls most of the countries of eastern Europe. There is a border between these countries and the west of Europe. Source C shows a look-out post on this border. Anyone trying to leave the Russian zone would be shot by the guards. This shows just how far apart the two sides have grown. They compete with each other in many ways to try to show the world how good they are. Both send men and women into space. Both send help to poorer countries to gain their support. Both try to do very well in sport: which country wins the most gold medals at the Olympic Games seems to be a very important question for the governments of the USA and the USSR.

Source C　*A lookout post on the border between East and West Germany*

The role of China in the Cold War

You might wonder why China, the other super-power, has not been mentioned in this chapter. This is because the phrase, 'the Cold War' is really only used to describe relations between the USA and the USSR. In 1949 Mao Zedong (sometimes spelt 'Tse-tung') took over as the new leader of China. He decided to concentrate on setting up a Communist government inside China itself. China did not have much contact with the world for the next 20 or 30 years. The Chinese did play a large part in the Korean War 1950–53 (see Chapter 9) and in the Vietnam War during the 1960s (see Chapter 14). In both these wars China became involved with both the USA and the USSR. China has also had continual quarrels with the USSR over where the borders should be between the two countries. On the whole though, the Chinese have kept themselves very much to themselves. It is the size and strength of China (see Chapter 1) that makes her a possible threat to the rest of the world.

4　Copy and complete a chart like this one by putting ticks in the correct places.

Event/ Fact	Countries it concerned or affected		
	USA	USSR	China
Look-out post on east/west border			
The Cold War			
The Korean War			
The Vietnam War			
Rivalry in sport aid to poorer countries			
Border disputes			

3 Capitalism v. Communism

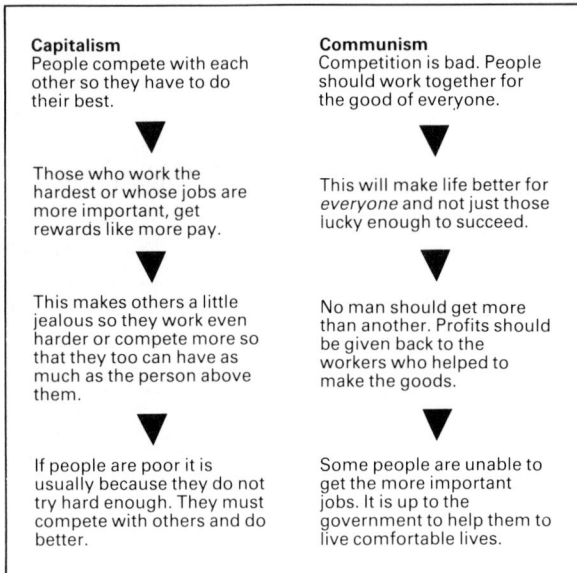

Capitalism
People compete with each other so they have to do their best.

▼

Those who work the hardest or whose jobs are more important, get rewards like more pay.

▼

This makes others a little jealous so they work even harder or compete more so that they too can have as much as the person above them.

▼

If people are poor it is usually because they do not try hard enough. They must compete with others and do better.

Communism
Competition is bad. People should work together for the good of everyone.

▼

This will make life better for *everyone* and not just those lucky enough to succeed.

▼

No man should get more than another. Profits should be given back to the workers who helped to make the goods.

▼

Some people are unable to get the more important jobs. It is up to the government to help them to live comfortable lives.

The diagram above tries to explain the two different ways that Communist countries like China and the USSR and capitalist countries like the USA think people should run their lives. The Cold War is partly about the fact that the two sides disagree about how things should be done. Each side wants to prove to the rest of the world that their own way works best.

---

1 **Which side (Communist or capitalist) would be most likely to believe each of the following in your opinion?**
   1 **Communism is wrong.**
   2 **Capitalism is wrong.**
   3 **People should compete with each other.**
   4 **Some people deserve more pay than others.**

   Which of the two ways (Communism or capitalism) most appeals to you? Explain why.

However, what people think *should* happen is not always the same as what *actually* happens.

What is life like in Communist and capitalist countries?

Here are three letters from 14-year-olds to pen-friends. They tell us a lot about life under the two systems. Which of the countries do you think you would most like to live in if you had a choice?

Read the letters first. Not *all* Russians, Chinese and Americans are exactly like the people you will learn about in these letters. But the letters will give you some idea of the different ways of life of the young people in these countries.

Honourable friend,

My name is Chiang. I am 14 years old. I have been at school since I was two. When I am 17 the Communist Party might allow me to work in a factory for two years. After that I hope to go to university to study politics. Politics is my favourite subject at school.

My mother and father work in a nearby factory. My father also serves on the factory committee that helps to run our local health centre. He would like to build a new building for the centre. In the end, the Communist Party will have to make the decision.

I have no brothers or sisters. The Party encourages families to have only one child. This is because there are already too many people living in China and we are trying to keep the population down. We live in a two-roomed flat which is quite comfortable. Soon we hope to have saved enough money to buy a television. I very much look forward to that. I would also like to own a bicycle. Then I could cycle to the Children's Palace on a Saturday. I go there to play my favourite sport which is table tennis. I have included a picture of three generations of our family having our mid-day meal together.

Yours respectfully,

CHIANG

Hello comrade,

My name is Leonid and I am 14 years old. I go to a special school which is for children who are good at maths. I have included a picture of our block of flats (my room is the one with an arrow pointing to it). We have *two* rooms to our flat. This is better than most people in Moscow. We share a kitchen with the family who live in the flat next door.

My mother and father work at a nearby factory. Nearly all women in the Soviet Union go out to work. We would like to have more money so that we could change our black and white television for a colour one. We *can* negotiate for higher wages but we are not allowed to strike, or work to rule, or picket, if we do not get all that we ask for. So we will have to wait a little longer.

It is now 7.30 pm and my father will soon be home with our supper. We will probably have some spiced sausage and bread. He is late which probably means he has had to queue for a long time or he has had to go to several shops to find some food on the shelves. If my parents were members of the Communist Party they would probably have a better flat and jobs. But we are better off than many.

At the weekend, I will probably play soccer which is my favourite sport. I hope to have the honour to represent my country one day.

Best wishes

Leonid

Hi,

That's me with the number 21 on my shirt during our High School football match last semester [term]. It'll soon be our three-month-long summer vacation and I hope to play a lot of football at summer camp.

Dad works in the car factory in Detroit. We live in a pretty small three-bedroomed house. It's OK but some of my friends rib me about not having enough space in my bedroom when they come for feasts and parties.

I reckon I'll be a motor mechanic when I leave school in two years' time. Dad's going to let me have his old car when I'm old enough and in the Fall he's going to teach me to drive.

I must dash now as I'm going to a computer club and then on to a disco as it's Friday night and there's no school tomorrow.

Cheers,

Nicky

---

2 In which country did the person live who, in your opinion:
   a had the best home to live in?
   b was most worried about food?
   c was most worried about money?
   d seemed to care most about his parents?

3 Choose either Chiang's or Leonid's letters and say what differences they show about each of the following compared to your own country:
   schools and school subjects   food
   favourite sports   housing
                                      possessions

4 The beginnings of the East/West split

You have seen in Chapter 3 that the two sides in the Cold War have different ideas about how people should be governed. Yet during the Second World War the USA and the USSR fought on the same side, against Germany. Source A shows what they agreed to do at the Yalta Conference in February 1945. Russia helped push German troops out of many of the countries east of Germany towards the end of the war. (See map, Source C.) Then at Potsdam in June 1945, Russia demanded more changes or more control over territories such as those shown in Source B below.

---

1 Look at Sources A, B and C below.
  a Which countries did the USSR gain control of after the Second World War?
  b What do you think the areas shaded like this ▦ are on the map, Source C?
  c Find out what countries 1, 2 and 3 are and say what happened to them.
  d Say what happened to Germany after the war. Who ruled over it?

---

2 Why do you think the USA and Britain allowed the USSR so much control over these countries after the war. Write down each of the following possible reasons and say whether this was a likely reason or not.

Reasons
1 Because they were grateful to Russia.
2 Because they trusted Russia.
3 Because they were afraid of war with Russia.

What were relations like between China, the USA and the USSR during these years?

China was at war against Japan between 1936 and 1945. In 1945 the USA dropped atomic bombs on Japan. The Japanese were no longer able to continue fighting. Two groups were trying to gain control in China at this time. They were:

1 the Nationalists led by Chiang Kai-shek, and
2 the Communists led by Mao Zedong.

Source A *Yalta, February 1945*

Britain, the USA and the USSR agreed:
1) Russia should be allowed to take land from eastern Poland and Poland would get some land from East Germany in return.
2) Germany should be divided into 4 zones controlled by Britain, France, the USA and the USSR (See inset in source B).
3) Russia agreed Britain could have some influence in Greece.
4) They all agreed to set up The United Nations organisation to keep world peace.

Source B *Potsdam, June 1945*

Britain, the USA and the USSR agreed:
1) Nazi war criminals should be rounded up and put on trial at Nuremburg.
2) Russia would be allowed to take land from Finland, Latvia, Estonia, Lithuania, Poland, Czechoslovakia and Rumania.

Source C *Europe after the Second World War (1945)*

The iron curtain: countries to the east were ruled by the USSR after 1945

The division of Germany and Austria into zones
B British
R Russian
F French
US American

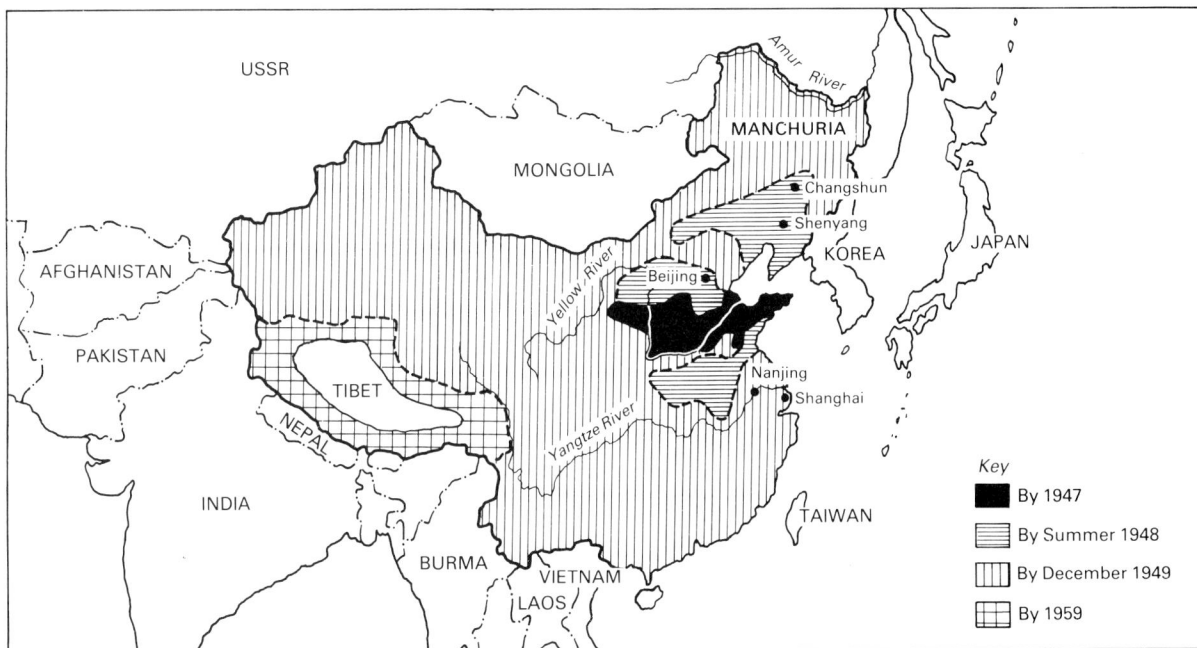

Source D *The Communist take-over of China*

The two sides fought a long war but by 1949 the Communists had gained control and Chiang Kai-shek had fled to the island of Taiwan. (Source D).

The new Chinese leader, Mao Zedong, was not very friendly towards *either* the USA *or* the USSR. This is why:
1 the USA had helped Chiang Kai-shek during the war in China.
2 the USSR had invaded Manchuria (see Source D), which was a part of China in 1945. A Manchurian described why the USSR might have invaded:

'The Russians seem to have had a very clear plan of action. They knew where all the industrial areas were, and had detailed plans for the removal of whole industrial plants with their machinery. To carry out their looting they needed all the skilled workers and experts they could lay their hands on. It took them several months to dismantle Ansham's machinery. It was then packed, numbered and crated.'

Source E

The leader of the USSR at this time was Stalin. He was a Communist and you might have expected him to help Mao Zedong, who was also a Communist; but he did not.

It is possible that Stalin feared that China might become a rival of the USSR and try to spread her own Communist ideas in the countries that the USSR had taken over.

3 Look at Source D. Which of the following phrases do you think best describes what the map shows?

  1 The Communists gained control very slowly in China.
  2 The Nationalists gained control very slowly in China.
  3 The Communists gained control quickly between 1947 and 1948.

4 a If you had been Mao Zedong in 1949 which of the following would you have done? Explain your choice.

  1 Made friends with the USA.
  2 Made friends with the USSR.
  3 Remained neutral.

  b Say why you would not have done the two you left out above.

5 a What does the writer of Source E think is the reason that the USSR invaded Manchuria?
  b What other things might you want to know before you trusted the evidence given by this writer? How would you decide whether it was true or not?

5 Russia and her satellites

If you were held prisoner in your home by a German soldier and a Russian set you free, what would you think? Would you be grateful to the Russian? You probably would be. But what would you think if the Russian said, 'I have freed you from a great evil. I therefore demand a reward and I want to take some things from your house. I am short of wood for instance, so I think I will have your dining room table'. You would probably think that he was going a bit far. You would no doubt be horrified if he then said that he wanted to send someone along to advise you how you should run your house from then onwards. This may seem far-fetched. But it was a bit like the situation in the countries of eastern Europe after the Second World War.

Stalin said that Russia had freed these countries from the Germans and that Russia therefore deserved a reward. He sent Russians to these countries and these Russians set up Communist governments that had to do what Russia wished. They had to give Russia valuable products like coal that they might have needed themselves. One-party governments were set up. This meant that the people could vote only for Communists: no other political parties were allowed.

These countries became known as Russian 'satellites' because they were like satellites in space that revolved around a big star. The USSR was the country that they revolved around.

---

1 Write down each of the following statements and then say whether or not you agree with them. Explain your answer by saying *why* you agree or disagree with each statement.

Statements
1 The Russians had freed eastern Europe from German control. This gave them the right to control these countries.
2 The Russians had used a lot of money freeing these countries from the Germans. They had a right to demand a reward.
3 It did not really matter what happened to other countries as long as Britain was safe.

---

2 What is happening in the photograph, Source A? Why don't you think the Polish people or government did anything to stop this?

Source A *Young boys in Poland being put to work by the Russians*

The Iron Curtain

This is how the British Prime Minister, Winston Churchill, described the situation in eastern Europe in 1945:

'From Stettin in the Baltic to Trieste in the Adriatic, an iron curtain has descended across the continent. Behind that line lie all the capitals of the ancient states of Central and Eastern Europe: Warsaw, Berlin, Prague, Vienna, Budapest, Belgrade, Bucharest and Sofia.'   **Source B**

Churchill made up the phrase 'the iron curtain'. He meant that the Russians had put up barbed wire and look-out posts along the border between western and eastern Europe. (See Chapter 2 Source C.) Thousands of people had been leaving the Russian satellite countries in the east and coming to live in the west because they thought that life in the west would be better. Stalin decided to stop this by making it impossible for people to cross the borders from east to west. This is why Churchill said there was an iron curtain. It was as if an iron barrier, impossible to cross, had been stretched across Europe. It is still there today.

3 Look at the extract from Churchill's speech. He mentions eight capital cities. Use an atlas to find out which countries they are the capitals of and write down the names of these countries under the heading 'Countries behind the iron curtain'.

4 Try to explain in your own words what 'the iron curtain' is. Can you think of a better phrase to describe it?

Czechoslovakia as an example

Russia often gained control in eastern European countries by first of all helping the existing Communist parties in those countries with funds to help them to win elections. Once these Communist parties got into power, Russia began to expect rewards for the help she had given them and Russia started to decide who would lead the countries and who would be in the governments. In the chart, Source C, you will see how the Communists gained control in Czechoslovakia.

Czechoslovakia was now firmly under Communist control. The Czech government of Alexandre Dubček tried to free itself from Russia in 1968 but Russian troops were sent in to restore a Communist government loyal to Russia. (See Chapter 10.)

5 Imagine you were a newspaper reporter living in Czechoslovakia at this time. Write an article about how the Russians exercised control over the country. Try to make comments about what good or bad things you think are happening, what you think the Czech people should do in order to keep their independence and why you think Masaryk might have been murdered.

1	1946	Communists won 114 out of 300 seats in the elections and helped to form a government.
2	July 1947	Stalin refused to allow the Czech government to accept help from the USA to rebuild Czech industry.
3	July 1947	Some non-Communist members of the government resigned as a protest against Russia's interference.
4	February 1948	Communists took over headquarters of other political parties and a Communist government was set up.
5	March 1948	Masaryk, the non-Communist foreign minister, was found dead. It was not clear whether he had been murdered or whether he committed suicide.
6	March 1948	Other non-Communists were forced to leave the government. Many were never seen again.
7	1950–52	Trials took place of many non-Communists. They were accused of treason and hundreds were executed.

Source C *(left) Communists in Czechoslovakia, (below) Masaryk. (Killed 1948)*

6 America courts Europe

The civil war in Greece, 1946–47

In 1946 a Greek Communist called Markos got an army together in Greece. This army began fighting against the army of the king of Greece, George II. George II's army was led by General Zervas. The British government had been giving help to the king of Greece but could not afford to do so any longer. Markos was being supplied with arms and ammunition by Albania and Bulgaria, both Communist countries. (See Chapter 5.)

The USA president, Harry S. Truman, was just beginning to believe in the 'Domino Theory'. (See Source A.) This was the theory or idea that if one country was taken over by Communists then the nearest country to it would be next, and that other bordering countries would then follow.

Source A *The Domino Theory*

1 **Look at Source A and Source B. copy the map, Source B and write the following paragraph by the side of it, filling in the missing words.**

Source B *The Mediterranean*

'In 1946 there was a civil war in _____. The Communists were being supplied with arms by _____ and _____. President Truman was worried because he thought that if Greece fell to the Communists then . . .' (complete the sentence).

2 **Copy Source A and call it 'The Domino Theory'. On the remaining dominoes, write in the names of the countries that would fall to Communism next if the Domino Theory was correct. Put them in the order in which they would fall.**

The Truman Doctrine

A doctrine is a set of ideas or beliefs. In March 1947 President Truman said the following, as a way of dealing with the problem of the spread of Communism:

'I believe that it must be the policy of the United States to support free people who are resisting attempted subjugation [take-over] by armed minorities or by outside pressures. I believe that our help should be primarily through economic and financial aid . . . The free peoples of the world look to us for support in maintaining their freedom. If Greece should fall, confusion and disorder might well spread throughout the Middle East. If we falter in our leadership, we may endanger the peace of the whole world.'

Source C

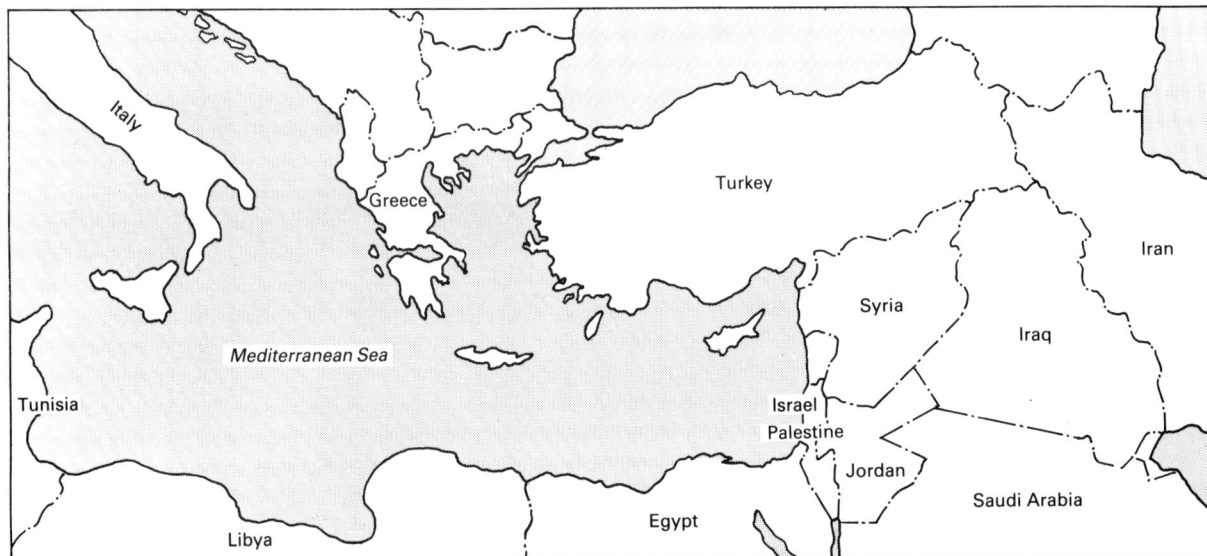

Source C *Harry S Truman, President of the USA*

3 Put a heading 'The Truman Doctrine 1947'.
Below are sentences. Some are true and some
are false. Write down only the ones that are
true.

Statements
1 President Truman was the president of the
USA in 1947.
2 'We will not oppose Communist take-overs in
Europe', Truman said.
3 Truman said that the USA would help people
fight Communism.
4 Truman said he would give countries weapons
to fight Communism.
5 Truman said he would give countries money
to help them fight against Communists.
6 Truman believed that the people of the world
did not care about the USA.
7 Truman believed that the USA should lead the
fight against Communism.

A Russian historian saw the Truman Doctrine
in a very different way. He wrote:

"The Truman Doctrine' ... meant in reality the
rearmament of Greece and Turkey and building
bases in these countries for American strategic

bombers. These actions were screened, of course, by
pompous pronouncements about defending democracy and peace.'

Source E

3 a Does this historian approve or disapprove
of the Truman doctrine?
b Which phrases led you to your answer?
c What is the writer accusing Truman of
really doing?
d Do you think the Russians had any need to
be afraid? Support your answer with some
evidence or reasons.

Marshall Aid: another form of help?

An Englishman in the 1830s once said, 'I defy you
to show me a revolutionary with a full stomach'.
President Truman also believed what this statement is trying to say; that is that people are more
likely to become revolutionaries when they are
poor or hungry and they blame their governments
for their situation. General George Marshall,
under Truman's direction, put forward the Marshall Plan in 1947. The plan simply said that the
USA would lend money to any country in Europe
that needed to build up their industries again
after the damage that had been caused to them
during the Second World War. Fourteen countries accepted the offer, including West Germany,
Austria, Greece and Britain. The money helped to
build factories and homes and to buy equipment
to get industry moving again. But Stalin refused
to allow any of the eastern European countries
under Russian control to accept money.

4 Below are some statements about Marshall
Aid. Put some under the heading 'Opinions
about Marshall Aid probably held by the USA'
and some under the heading 'Opinions about
Marshall Aid probably held by the USSR'.

Statements
1 It was a way of gaining influence in Europe
before the Communists did.
2 It was a way of increasing American trade by
persuading countries to buy American goods.
3 It was an attempt to help countries to rebuild
their industries.
4 It was a way of finding places near Russia on
which to put bomber bases.

5 What do *you* think the Americans were really
trying to achieve with the Truman Doctrine
and Marshall Aid?

17

7 The siege of Berlin, 1948–49

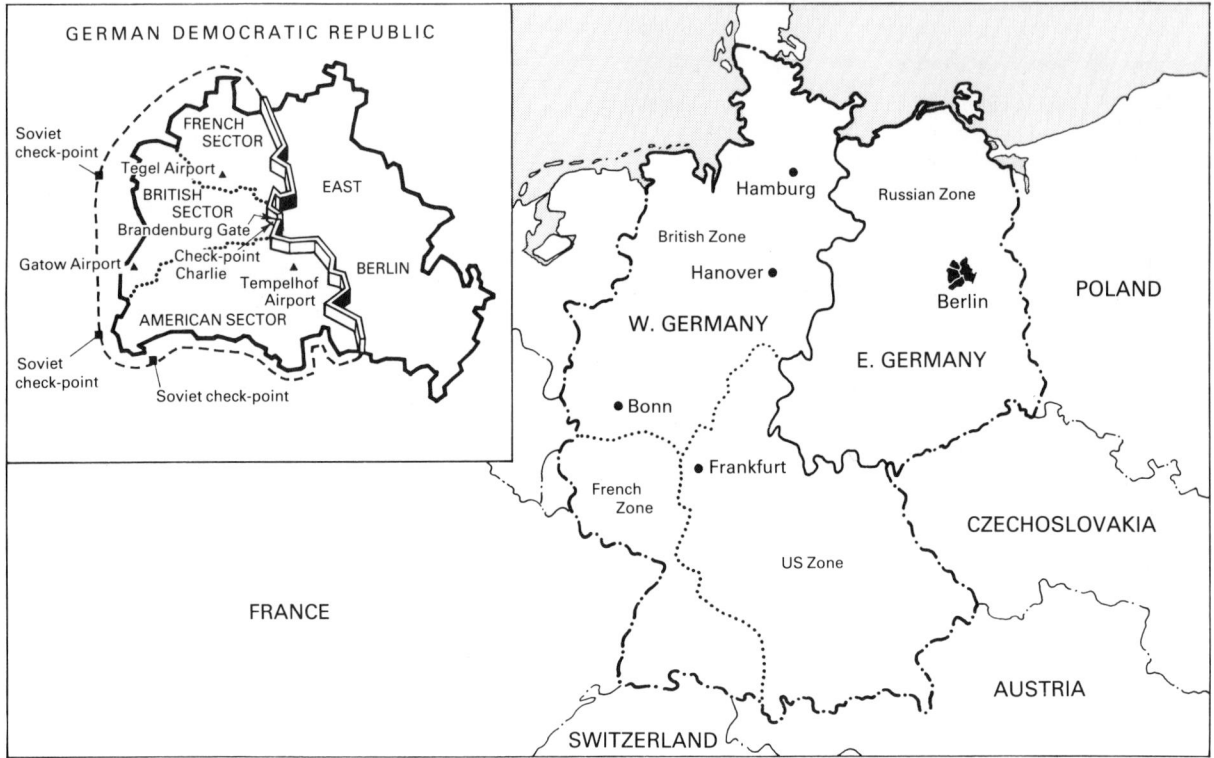

Source A *The division of Germany, June 1948*

If you look carefully at Source A you will be able to answer question 1. This will help you to understand the situation that existed in Germany in June 1948.

---

1 **Write out the following paragraph. Where there are two choices of phrases or words divided by a / you must write down only the one that you think is correct.**

Berlin 1948
In 1947 Germany was divided into West Germany and East Germany. The Russians/Americans controlled East Germany whereas West/East Germany was controlled by Russia/America for a time but became a free democratic country. But Berlin (the capital of West Germany) was in fact inside West/East Germany. The city of Berlin itself was also divided. The Americans/Russians controlled the eastern half of the city and the other half was controlled by Britain, France and America.

You can see from what you have written in the answer to question 1 that West Berlin was sur-

rounded by Communist or Russian-controlled East Germany. It was like an island of freedom surrounded by a sea of Communist-controlled country. In June of 1948 Britain, France and the USA introduced a new currency or money system

Source B *A crossing point between two zones in West Berlin*

into their half of Berlin. The Russian leader, Stalin, thought that they were trying to let West Berlin become rich while the eastern part of the city became poor.

Britain, France and America then started to set up a new constitution or government for West Berlin as if they wanted to separate it from the East. The Russians then did the same thing in East Berlin. It was almost as if two cities were trying to live in the same space.

Soon, the currency of West Berlin became more popular than that of East Berlin. So, on 26 June 1948 Stalin cut off all road, rail, river and canal links between West Germany and West Berlin. This meant that the people of West Berlin were now completely surrounded by the Communist-controlled East Germany. Stalin hoped that the people of West Berlin would run out of food and agree in the end to be ruled directly by Russia just like the rest of East Germany. Power supplies were also cut and as the *Daily Express* wrote on 9 July 1948:

'Two million people in West Berlin settle down in gloom tonight. There will be only four hours electric light a day; half in the morning and half at night. Wives and children in the French sector of Berlin have been advised to leave as soon as possible owing to the food shortages.'

Source C

---

2 What *two* things did America, Britain and France do in West Berlin that annoyed Stalin?

---

3 What did Stalin do on 26 June 1948 and what did he hope to achieve?

It would have been easy for Britain, France and the USA to let Stalin have control of the whole of Berlin. After all, it did seem a bit odd that Russia should control all the territory around Berlin itself but not the western part of the city of Berlin. But many leaders in the Western world believed in the Domino Theory (see Chapter 6) and felt that if they let Stalin get away with seizing West Berlin then he might not just stop there. He might decide to try to take over West Germany and other countries in western Europe.

So, between 26 June 1948 and 12 May 1949 British, French and American planes made half-a-million flights from airfields in West Germany. They took $2\frac{1}{2}$ million tonnes of supplies to the people of West Berlin to help them to withstand the siege. On many days planes were taking off

after each other at 90 second intervals. General Lucius Clay, the main organiser, said:

'Berlin under blockade was like a besieged city with only one supply line linking it to the western world, the airlift bringing food, clothes, coal, raw materials and medicine to the $2\frac{1}{2}$ million men, women and children in its western sectors. 'Operation Vittles' grew steadily. On the record day it delivered almost 13000 tons to our three airports.'

Source D

On 12 May 1949 Stalin called off the blockade. It was obvious that the Western world was not going to let West Berlin come under Russian control. The Berlin airlift had worked and the West had won this latest battle in the Cold War (see Chapter 2).

---

4 a Describe what is happening in the photograph, Source E, and say why it is happening.

 b What has the Domino Theory got to do with the Berlin Blockade?

Source E *The one millionth sack of coal being lifted from a US aeroplane in 1948*

8 Friends and enemies: superpower alliances

Source A *A street corner gang in an American city*

You have probably seen, or perhaps been a member, of a street gang like the one in the photograph, Source A. Why do you think people join gangs like these? Is it because they want to protect themselves from other such gangs? Or is it that they want to cause trouble and attack others? Perhaps it is a little of both. In any case, what has all this got to do with superpower rivalry?

It is important to know what reasons people give for joining with other groups. In 1949 NATO (the North Atlantic Treaty Organisation) was formed. (See Source C.) The USA joined 11 other countries in this group or alliance. The main aim of such an alliance was for the 12 countries to defend themselves in case the USSR decided to try to spread Communism. One of the clauses of the treaty that set up NATO said that:

'an armed attack against one or more of them in Europe or North America shall be considered an attack against them all.'

1 a On an outline map of the world, mark on the countries who became members of NATO by using a coloured pencil to shade them in on the map.
  b According to the clause from the treaty quoted above, what do you think was supposed to happen if one of the members of NATO was attacked?

2 How do you think the leaders of the USSR felt when NATO was formed? Choose *one* of the words or phrases below and explain why you think they might have felt this way.

ANGRY   WORRIED   PLEASED
THREATENED   SURROUNDED
NOT BOTHERED

Which words did the other people in your class pick and what did they say about them?

This is what Stalin, the leader of the USSR said about NATO when it was formed:

'The Soviet government did everything it could to prevent the world from being split into two military blocks. It appealed to the countries who might participate in such an organisation to hold back from joining an anti-Soviet alliance ... the Soviet Union issued a special statement analysing in detail the grave consequences affecting the entire international situation that would follow from the establishment of a military alliance of the Western powers.

All these warnings failed, however, and the North Atlantic Alliance came into being.'

Source B

3 Read Source B and then say:
  a what the Soviet Union accuses the USA of doing.
  b whether you think the view is justified or not.
  c what you would expect the USSR to do next.

The Warsaw Pact, 1953

The USSR certainly felt threatened by NATO. So, in 1953, they formed their own military organisation known as the Warsaw Pact (because the treaty was signed in Warsaw, the capital of Poland). The Warsaw Pact was formed mainly because the USSR was afraid of being surrounded by countries who were members of NATO. Fear of each other was once again making relations between these two superpowers very bad. NATO was formed because the Americans were afraid of Russian attacks, and the Warsaw Pact was

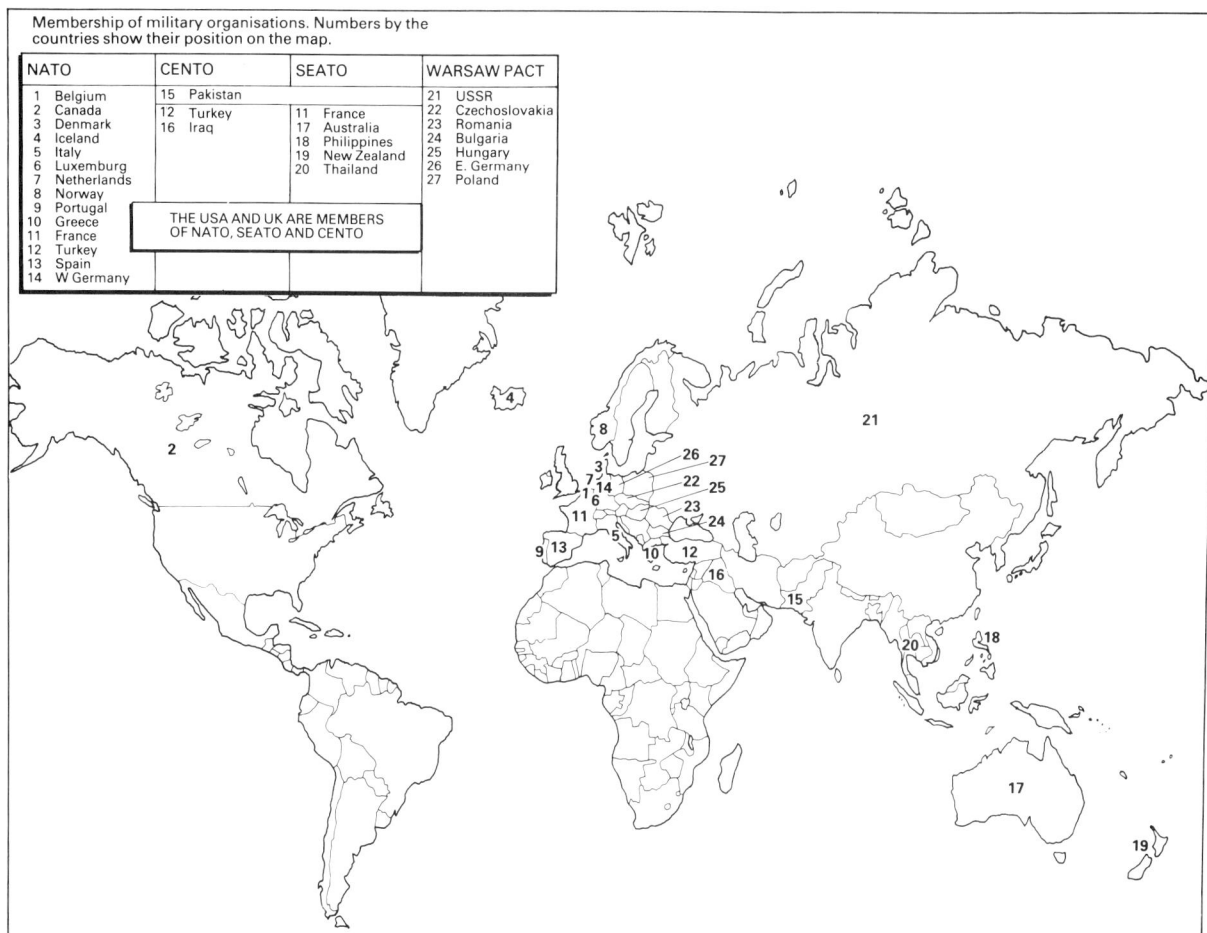

Membership of military organisations. Numbers by the countries show their position on the map.

NATO	CENTO	SEATO	WARSAW PACT
1 Belgium 2 Canada 3 Denmark 4 Iceland 5 Italy 6 Luxemburg 7 Netherlands 8 Norway 9 Portugal 10 Greece 11 France 12 Turkey 13 Spain 14 W Germany	15 Pakistan 12 Turkey 16 Iraq	11 France 17 Australia 18 Philippines 19 New Zealand 20 Thailand	21 USSR 22 Czechoslovakia 23 Romania 24 Bulgaria 25 Hungary 26 E. Germany 27 Poland

THE USA AND UK ARE MEMBERS OF NATO, SEATO AND CENTO

Source C   *Membership of military organisations*

formed because the Russians were afraid of NATO.

---

4   Use a second colour to shade in the Warsaw Pact countries on your outline map of the world and show this in your key.

Fear and suspicion continues: SEATO and CENTO

In 1954 SEATO (South East Asia Treaty Organisation) was formed in Manila, the capital of the Philippines. This, like NATO, was supposed to help the countries who joined (see Source C) protect themselves against Communism. The same was true of CENTO (Central Nations Treaty Organisation) that was formed in 1959 in Ankara, the capital of Turkey. CENTO was an attempt to prevent Communism from spreading to the Middle East. The CENTO treaty also allowed the USA to place missiles in Turkey. They could

easily destroy many Russian cities by firing these missiles. This became a major problem during the Cuban Missile Crisis in 1962 (see Chapter 13).

There has not been a major war between the Warsaw Pact countries and the members of NATO, SEATO and CENTO. This makes some people say that these alliances have actually helped to prevent war between the superpowers. On the other hand, NATO and the Warsaw Pact *are* increasing their arms (see Source A in Chapter 1) and this in itself could be a real danger to peace. They see each other as enemies.

---

5   Complete your map by using two more colours to shade in the members of SEATO and CENTO and show this on your key.

---

6   Try to say in what ways 'Fear of each other' was once again making relations between the superpowers worse.

---

9 Superpower conflict: the Korean War 1950–53

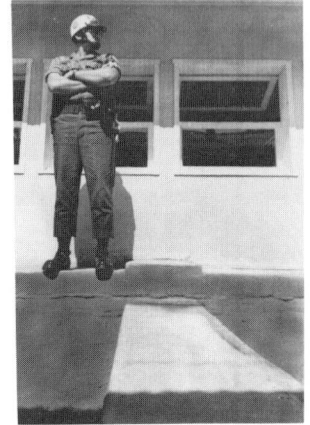

Source A *The conference room on the border between North and South Korea. The border runs through the table, inside, and along the concrete strip on the outside (see above).*

Every year since 1953 representatives of North Korea's Communist government enter the building shown in Source A from the north. They sit down around one side of a table and wait. Representatives of the South Korean government then enter through another doorway and sit down around the opposite side of the table. The building is on the border between North and South Korea (the 38th parallel of latitude, see the map, Source B) and the border runs through the middle of the table. Therefore, the representatives never actually have to cross the border in order to talk to each other. They meet every year to try to work out a peace treaty for a war between the two countries that went on from 1950 to 1953. On 17 July 1953 both sides agreed to an armistice which means that they agreed to stop fighting. But no peace treaty has ever been signed. As recently as 1978 it was discovered that the North Koreans were digging tunnels under the border to try to get troops into the South. The South Koreans dug their own tunnels to intercept them and stop this from happening.

1 a **Why do delegates of North and South Korea meet every year?**
  b **What is an armistice?**
  c **What happened in 1978 in North Korea and why?**

So, how has this strange situation come about? It was because of a war that involved all *three* superpowers, the USA, the USSR *and* China.

Source B shows the position of Korea in relation to China. The story really began in 1945 at the end of the Second World War. North Korea surrendered to the Russians and South Korea to the USA. The 38th parallel was the border between them. It was intended that one day a single government would rule the whole of Korea. But this never happened and by 1949 a Communist government was ruling the North and a government backed by the USA was ruling the South.

On 25 June 1950 the North Koreans, supplied with arms by Russia, attacked the South in an attempt to take over the whole of Korea. The next

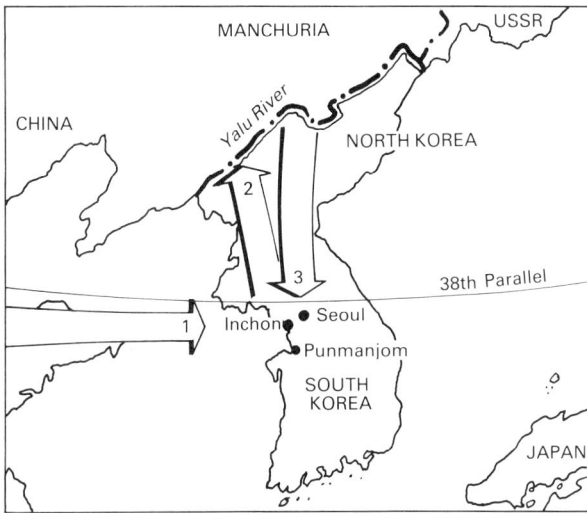

Source B *The Korean War, 1950–53*

c Draw an arrow like this ⇨ coming from the West and pointing at Inchon. Inside the arrow write '1.September 1950, UN troops land and push Communists back to 38th parallel'.

day the Security Council of the United Nations (see Chapter 1) ordered the North Koreans to withdraw. When they refused to do this, the UN sent a peace-keeping force, made up of men from 16 countries, to support South Korea. Most of the troops were American and they were led by United States' General George McArthur. The USSR delegates were not present at the Security Council at the time as they had walked out in protest at the entry of China to the United Nations. They were therefore unable to stop the UN from sending troops to South Korea.

In September 1950 the troops landed at Inchon and soon captured Seoul back from the Communists. Soon afterwards they had pushed the Communists back to the 38th parallel. It seemed as if their task had been completed.

2 Draw the map, Source B. Put the following information onto it.
a Shade North Korea in grey and show in your key that this was a Communist controlled country in 1949.
b Leave South Korea white and show in the key who backed the South Korean government.

Source C
General McArthur

The war continues

The USA, however, decided not to leave things as they were but to extend the war. With the backing of the UN they invaded North Korea and tried to push the Communists back beyond the Yalu river and into China.

3 a Draw a second arrow on your map like this ⇨. Write inside it, '2.UN troops invade North Korea'.
   b Do you think they were right in your opinion to invade the North in order to rid Korea of Communists? Say why.

Enter China, October 1950

When the UN troops reached the Yalu river McArthur wanted to carry the war further and invade China. President Truman sacked McArthur and replaced him with General Ridgeway. But, by the end of October 1950 half-a-million Chinese troops were inside North Korea helping to fight off the UN forces. By January 1951 the UN troops had been pushed back to the 38th parallel again.

4 Show the above information on your map inside arrow 3.

Why did Korea matter?

Bitter fighting continued along the 38th parallel until the signing of the armistice on 17 July 1953. President Truman had even talked of using nuclear weapons at one stage. Since the signing of the armistice Korea has been two countries divided by the 38th parallel. But Communism *had* been contained ('held back') again. Even more important perhaps was the fact that the Chinese had proved that their massive manpower could be made to be a very powerful weapon. They had intervened in a major war and effected the result. The rest of the world would have to take more notice of China.

5 Look at Source C. Explain what part this man played in the Korean War. Why was he dismissed and do you agree with the reason why he was dismissed? Say why.

23

10 Containment from without and within

'Containment' was the name of the policy the USA was taking to try to hold back Communism. This was what the USA was trying to do in Korea in 1950–53. (See Chapter 9.)

---

1 Look back over the last nine chapters. Which of the following do you think were attempts at containment? Say in what ways.

The division of Germany, 1945; the Truman Doctrine; Marshall Aid; the Berlin Airlift, 1948; NATO, 1949; the Warsaw Pact, 1955; The Korean War, 1950–53.

'Containment' inside the Eastern Bloc

The USSR did not, of course, have to contain Communism. *They* wanted to spread Communism. But they did have to contain a great deal of unrest inside the countries they had taken over. Some of this unrest seemed to be a protest against Russian control. From 1940 to 1952 the USSR leaders

Source A

Country	Russian occupation	Leaders of take overs	Fate
Estonia, Lativia and Lithuania	1940		
Poland	1944	Boleslaw Bierut Josef Cyrankiewicz	(Retired 1954) (Replaced by Gomulka 1956)
East Germany (GDR)	1945	Wilhelm Pieck Otto Grotewohl	(Replaced by Ulbricht, 1954)
Czechoslovakia	1945 (temporarily)	Klement Gottwald Zdenek Fierlinger Rudolf Slanksy	(d. 1953) Executed 1952
Hungary	1944	Erno Gero Matyas Rakosi Laslo Rajk	Replaced in 1956 Executed in 1949
Rumania	1944	Anna Pauker Gheorghiu Dej	Removed 1952 (d. 1965)
Yugoslavia	1945	Josif Tito Milovan Djilas	(d. 1980) Removed 1954
Bulgaria	1945	Georgi Dimitrov Traicho Kostov	Died Moscow 1950 Executed 1949

(From *Modern World Affairs Made Simple* by Peter King)

carried out a number of 'purges' to get rid of leaders in the Eastern Bloc countries who disagreed with the way Russia was trying to dominate them. Some were removed and sent to prison camps but some were simply executed. (See Source A.)

---

2 Draw a bar graph to show what happened to eastern European leaders between 1940 and 1956 (see Source A). Use these words as your headings for each of the sections of your bar graph:

RETIRED DIED EXECUTED REPLACED OR REMOVED

What does the graph tell you about the attitude of the Russian leaders to people who criticised them?

Here are three more detailed case studies of what happened to countries who tried to shake off the control of the USSR.

Case study 1: Hungary, 1956

In 1956 Hungarian people attacked Russian tanks in the streets of Budapest, the capital. The protests were against the prime minister, Rakosi, who had employed a secret police force known as the AVH to torture political prisoners and anyone who disagreed with him. The Russians moved their tanks away for a time during the protests and Rakosi fled the country. Imre Nagy (pro-

Source B *An AVH suspect is tortured*

nounced Nodge) became prime minister. He began to introduce more freedoms, such as allowing writers to criticise the government and political discussions to take place on the radio. Other parties besides the Communists were also allowed to exist. Nagy also disbanded the hated AVH.

But then Nagy went too far for the Russians by saying that he no longer wanted Hungary to be a member of the Warsaw Pact. On 4 November 1956 the Russian tanks moved into Budapest again and killed over 25 000 rioters. Nagy was arrested and two years later he was hanged. A Communist government was set up again and the Hungarian uprising had failed.

The rest of the world did nothing. This was partly because the other major powers were involved with another crisis, the Suez Crisis (see Chapter 15) and partly because the USA and China did not want to risk war by interfering in a part of the world that they thought was none of their business.

Source C *Lek Walesa, leader of Solidarity*

party had to allow it; the trade union was called 'Solidarity'. But the leaders of Poland's government were summoned to Moscow for a conference. When they returned they set up Martial Law in Poland. Among other things this meant that people were not allowed on the streets after a certain time of night. Lek Walesa and other leaders of Solidarity have been arrested several times and the union's offices were raided and people who worked there were taken away. The union is now banned. The Poles, like the Hungarians and the Czechs, had failed to win their freedom and the Russians had managed to 'contain' unrest in the Eastern Bloc.

---

3 a **What caused the Hungarian uprising in 1956?**
   b **What did Nagy try to do and what was the result?**
   c **Do you think the other world powers should have stopped the Russians? Say why.**

Case study 2: Czechoslovakia, 1968

During the 1960s the Czech people began to demand the right to free speech and to have a choice between political parties. In 1968 Alexander Dubček (pronounced Dubcheck) became leader of the Czech Communist party. He allowed more freedom of speech and Russia feared that the other Warsaw Pact countries might start to ask for such freedom. In August 1968 troops from Russia and other Eastern Bloc countries entered Czechoslovakia and took control. Dubček was arrested and taken to Moscow. The Russians refused to take their troops away until all other parties except the Communist party were banned. By 1969 the Communist party had got things back to 'normal'. Freedom of speech was not allowed again and Dubček was dismissed as party leader.

Case study 3: Poland, 1981

By 1981 Lek Walesa (see photograph) had set up a trade union in the shipyards in the Polish city of Gdansk. Trade unions were illegal in Poland but so many people joined it that the Communist

---

4 **Complete the following table by ticking in the right place the things that happened in the three case studies.**

	Hungary 1956	Czechoslovakia 1968	Poland 1981
Protests against secret police			
New more liberal leader takes over			
Freedom of speech given			
New political parties allowed			
Russian tanks being brought in			
The new leader being replaced by another			
A trade union formed			
The people win their revolution			
The other countries do something to help			
The other countries do nothing to help			

11 The Thaw, 1952–61

In 1953 John Foster Dulles, the USA Secretary of State for foreign affairs said:

'We shall never have a secure peace or happy world so long as Soviet communism dominates one third of all the peoples that there are, and is trying to extend its rule to many others.

Therefore we must always have in mind the liberation of these captive people.'

Source A

1 **Rewrite Dulles' statement in your own words and then say whether you think it would improve or worsen relations between the USA and USSR. Explain why.**

Six years later in 1959 President Nikita Khrushchev of the USSR agreed that the USA and the USSR would only learn to agree when 'shrimps learnt to fly' (in other words, never). But he was not so extreme in his comments about how the two superpowers could get along. In a speech called 'On peaceful coexistence' he said:

'We communists believe that the idea of communism will be victorious throughout the world, just as it has been in our country, in China and in many states. Many will probably disagree with us. It is their right to think so. We may argue, we may disagree with each other. The main thing is to keep

to [arguing] without resorting to arms in order to prove that one is right.'

Source B

2 **Put Khrushchev's words into your own words. Which of the following three phrases do you think best sums up the idea of peaceful coexistence? Explain your answer.**

1 **Coexistence is the idea that the USA and the USSR should fight each other.**
2 **Coexistence is the idea that the USSR and the USA should become the best of friends.**
3 **Coexistence is the idea that the USA and the USSR should live side by side peacefully even though they do not agree.**

'The Thaw'

Nikita Khrushchev was the leader of Russia from 1953 until 1964. You have seen in the previous chapter that he did not allow the Hungarian people to have the freedom they wanted. In foreign policy however, he brought about an era known as 'The Thaw' during which relations between the USSR and other major powers were warmer or better than before. It was called The Thaw because it was as if the Cold War was getting a bit warmer, like ice that melts when the temperature gets warmer. On page 27 is a list of things that Khrushchev did that have been seen as part of a 'thaw' in relations between the USSR and the other countries of the world.

Source C *Khrushchev on his visit to the USA*

(1) Khrushchev visits Yugoslavia, 1953

Just after the Second World War Yugoslavia had argued with the USSR because she did not want to accept Soviet rule even though she was a Communist country. Stalin frequently called Tito, the Yugoslav leader, a traitor. But in 1953 Khrushchev visited Tito and apologised, saying that the blame for the argument was Stalin's and saying that Russia and Yugoslavia could follow separate paths to Communism. This was certainly an improvement in relations between the two countries.

(2) Poland, 1956

There was a series of riots in Poland in 1956 rather like those in Hungary. Khrushchev allowed the leader, Gomulka, to return to power rather than risk losing control of a country so close to the West.

(3) Khrushchev visits Britain, 1959

In 1959 Khrushchev visited Britain in an effort to improve relations between the two countries.

(4) Khrushchev visits the USA, 1959

The most important visit of all was in 1959 when Khrushchev visited the USA for talks with president Eisenhower. This was the first time that the leaders of the world's two most powerful nations had met since the end of the Second World War. The two men talked about how to improve relations between their countries.

The Thaw ends: the Summit Conference, 1960

In 1960 Khrushchev suggested that Russia should meet the other nations of the world at a summit

Source D *Here is an American U2 spy plane like the one shot down over Russia in 1960. Do you think Khrushchev was justified in the action he took over this incident?*

conference in Paris. He wanted to reach an agreement with the West in order to avoid a nuclear war. Two weeks before the conference was due to take place, the Russians shot down an American U2 spy plane. Khrushchev was furious that the Americans had been spying on Russia at a time when he was trying to improve relations between them. He refused to attend the conference until he got an apology. Eisenhower refused to apologise and the conference broke down. Relations between the USA and the USSR seemed to be getting worse even though Krushchev had said he wanted them to get better.

3 Below you will see a thermometer drawn vertically. The temperatures at the bottom are meant to be cold and represent times when relations between the USA and the USSR were cold or bad. The further up you go, the warmer the temperature and the better the relations. Copy the diagram. Put an X in each column depending on how hot or cold you think relations between the two countries were when the event mentioned in the column was taking place.

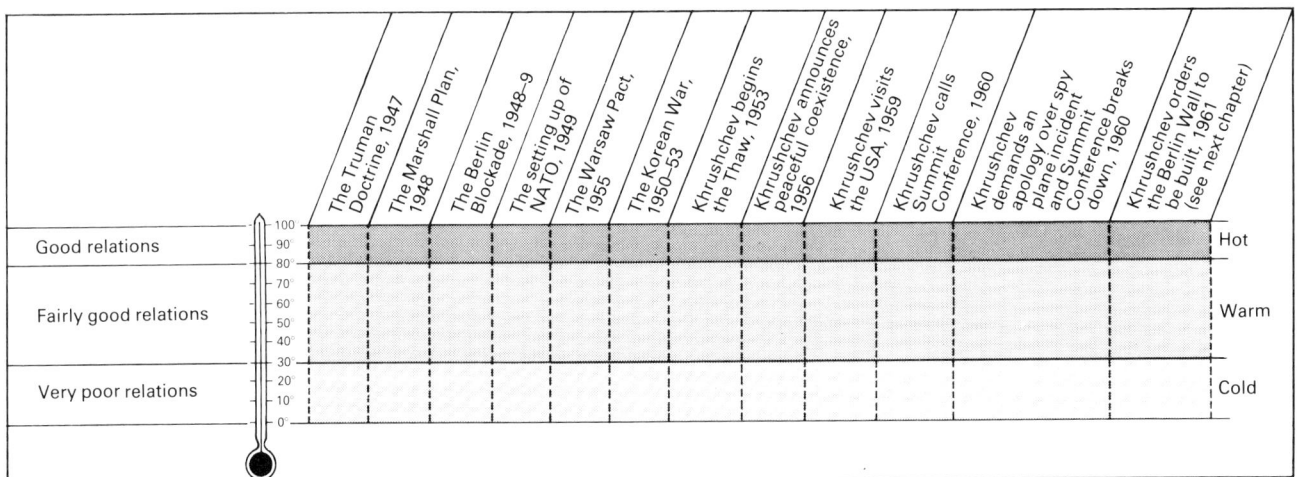

	The Truman Doctrine, 1947	The Marshall Plan, 1948	The Berlin Blockade, 1948–9	The setting up of NATO, 1949	The Warsaw Pact, 1955	The Korean War, 1950–53	Khrushchev begins the Thaw, 1953	Khrushchev announces peaceful coexistence, 1956	Khrushchev visits the USA, 1959	Khrushchev calls Summit Conference, 1960	Khrushchev demands an apology over spy plane incident and Summit Conference breaks down, 1960	Khrushchev orders the Berlin Wall to be built, 1961 (see next chapter)	
Good relations													Hot
Fairly good relations													Warm
Very poor relations													Cold

12 The Berlin Wall, 1961

You will see from your answer to question 3 in the previous chapter that relations between the USA and the USSR improved during the 1950s. But by 1961 they had reached a low point again. On 13 August 1961 relations became worse than they had been since the end of the Second World War in 1945. It was during the night of 12–13 August 1961 that the USSR began the building of the Berlin Wall.

What *is* the Berlin Wall?

Source A shows East German workmen building the wall in 1961 and Sources D and E are diagrams showing how the wall has been extended since then. It is a wall that goes all the way around West Berlin. You may remember that West Berlin was a city inside East Germany but not under the control of East Germany or the USSR. (See Chapter 7.) The magazine *The Economist* described the situation six days after the first temporary wall was built:

Source A *German workers being forced to build the Berlin Wall*

'About two o'clock last Sunday morning ... a strong east German paramilitary force moved up to the sector boundary between East and West Berlin. When Berlin awoke the sector frontier was effectively closed and movement from the Eastern side was at a halt.

The East German forces ... were equipped with enough barbed wire, concrete road blocks and digging equipment to seal the frontier completely and this they did with the exception of thirteen control points. During the night heavy concentrations of tanks, armoured troop carriers and trucks carrying hoses and tear gas took up position at these and other key points just behind the frontier. Much of the fifty five kilometres of sector boundary consists of canal or railway. When it is not, and houses in the east face directly across the frontier, police have occupied basements or walled off doors. Since Sunday a few bold spirits have hit the headlines by swimming canals or creeping through the wire at night, but they number only a few hundred altogether and each day the barrier becomes more elaborate.'
Source B

1 a **Look at the photograph, Source A. What makes you think that the workmen are reluctant to build the wall?**
   b **Who ordered that the wall should be built?**
   c **Which people could not go through the wall: East Berliners or West Berliners?**

2 **Using Sources A, D and E and the extract from the *Economist* write a list of at least ten difficulties that East Berliners would face if they tried to cross the wall, for example, dogs, tanks and border guards.**

Why was the Berlin Wall built?

The official view of the Communist-controlled East German government about why the wall was built is this:

'In no other part of the world are so many spies of foreign states to be found as in West Berlin. Nowhere else can they act with such freedom. These spies are smuggling agents into the GDR [German Democratic Republic—the Russian name for East Germany], inciting sabotage and provoking riots and demonstrations.'
Source C

In a famous speech made in 1962 the USA president, Kennedy, gave a different opinion about why the wall was built:

'Democracy may not be perfect. But we never had to put up walls to keep our people in.'

3 a **Why do (i) the GDR and (ii) the USA say the Berlin Wall was built?**
   b **Which of the two explanations do you most agree with? Say why.**

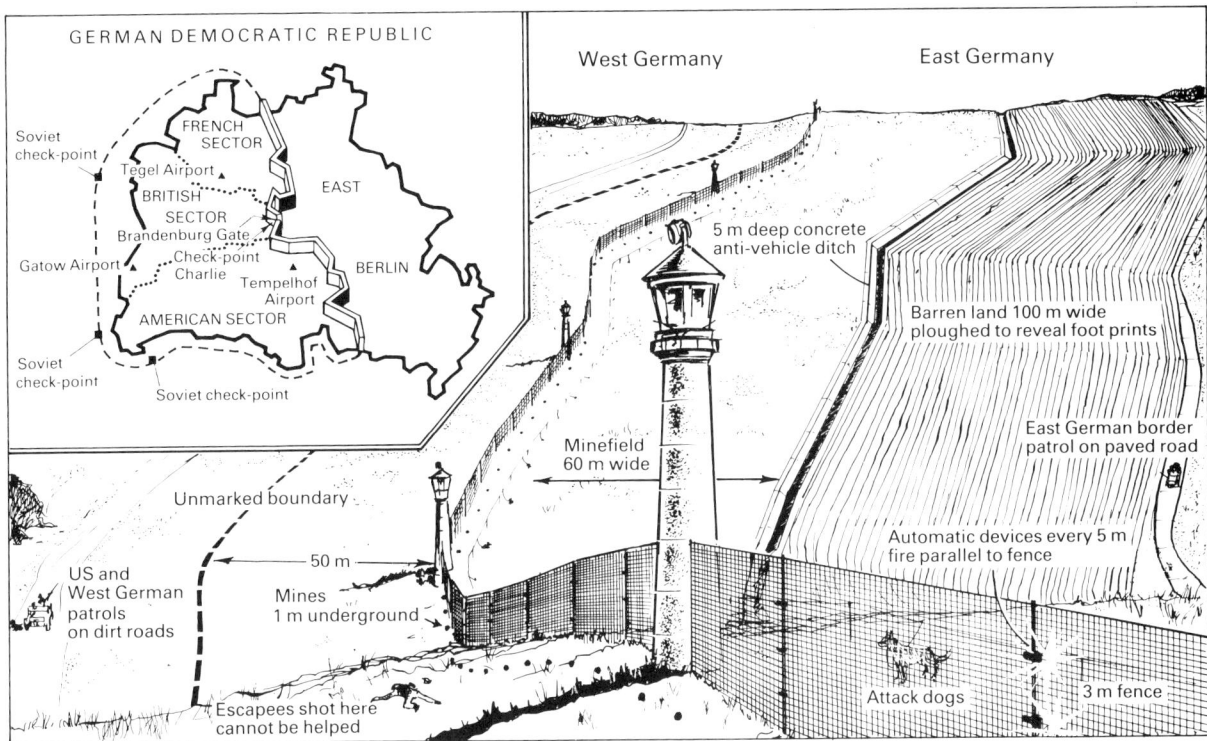

Source D and E *The Berlin Wall, 1961*

Labels within the diagram:

GERMAN DEMOCRATIC REPUBLIC
- Soviet check-point
- FRENCH SECTOR
- Tegel Airport
- BRITISH SECTOR
- EAST
- Brandenburg Gate
- Gatow Airport
- Check-point Charlie
- BERLIN
- Tempelhof Airport
- AMERICAN SECTOR
- Soviet check-point
- Soviet check-point

West Germany — East Germany
- 5 m deep concrete anti-vehicle ditch
- Barren land 100 m wide ploughed to reveal foot prints
- Minefield 60 m wide
- East German border patrol on paved road
- Automatic devices every 5 m fire parallel to fence
- Unmarked boundary
- US and West German patrols on dirt roads
- 50 m
- Mines 1 m underground
- Attack dogs
- 3 m fence
- Escapees shot here cannot be helped

Escape across the wall

The *Economist* article quoted on p. 28 mentions that hundreds of people escaped across the wall during the first few days after it was built. The frontier has been strengthened since then, as you can see from Sources D and E. Nevertheless, people still do try to escape through the wall to reach the West because they do not like life under the East German Communist government. People who visit East Berlin from the West usually find it a pretty miserable place. There are always long queues at shops for things such as bread or fruit and often there is not enough food to go around. There are no fashionable clothes on sale and there are only two department stores; although none of the East Berliners earn enough money to be able to buy anything in them. The people can only vote for one political party, the Communists; all others are banned. People are not allowed to criticise too much what their government says or does. Strikes are illegal. East German border guards always work in pairs so that if one of them is thinking of escaping the other one can arrest him.

Nevertheless, some East Germans have escaped across the wall by tying up their partners. Wolf Quasner, a West Berliner, has organised many escapes for people since 1961. He got six men through the wall by disguising them as nuns, and several people through by hiding them under false floors in cars or in packing cases. One man got through by dressing in the costume of an old English sheep dog and another dressed up as a sheep and crossed the border with a flock of sheep going to market in the West. One family escaped over the wall in a hot air balloon. But since that time the East Germans shoot down all hot air balloons crossing from East to West. Attempted escapes do not usually work because the border guards are well trained and on the look out.

The wall still stands. It is a division between the Eastern and Western worlds that can easily be seen and understood by anyone who visits Berlin.

4 Imagine you are living in East Berlin. Write a story or diary about how you plan to escape to the West. Try to include the following information:
   why you want to escape;
   details of your plans;
   your fears about what might happen;
   a description of what actually happens.
   (Remember, at least 9 out of 10 attempted escapes end in failure.)

13　The Cuba Crisis, 1962

Just over a year after the building of the Berlin Wall (see Chapter 12) relations between the USA and the USSR reached an even lower point. They became involved in a conflict over Cuba (see Source A) that nearly led to a war between them.

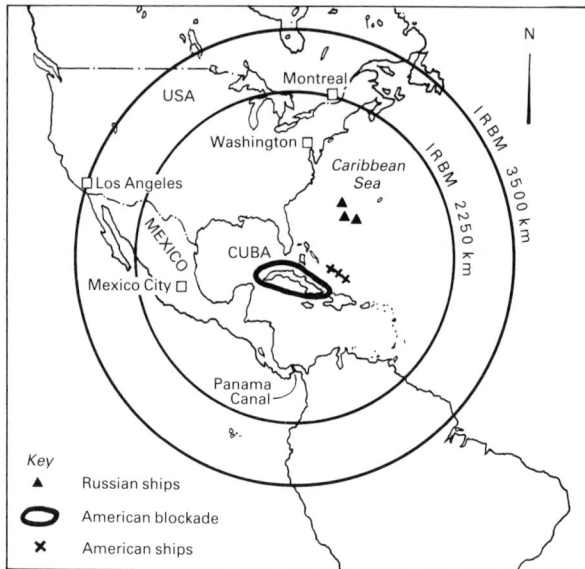

Source A　*The threat that missiles on Cuba could pose (IRBM: Intermediate Range Ballistic Missiles)*

Before 1959 Cuba had been friendly with the USA and had traded with her (see Source B). But in 1959 Fidel Castro, a Communist, took over as leader of Cuba. President John F. Kennedy of the USA did not like having a Communist country so close to the USA and so in 1961 he sent some soldiers to try to take over the island of Cuba. The soldiers landed at the Bay of Pigs in Cuba but failed to get rid of Castro. Castro was angry and he began trading with the USSR and becoming more friendly with Khrushchev who was the leader of the USSR.

Source B

	Direction of Cuban Trade 1955–60			
	1955	1960	1955	1960
	Exports		Imports	
USA	67.5%	56.7%	73.6%	47.4%
EEC	5.9	6.4	7.4	10.0
UK	1.2	3.2	2.3	4.4
Sino-Soviet area	6.6	18.7	0.2	16.5
USSR	6.1	16.7	0.0	13.8

The Cuban Missile Crisis, October 1962

On Tuesday 16 October 1962 some photographs, including Sources C and D, were shown to John F. Kennedy. They showed Russian ships carrying missiles towards Cuba and Russian-built missile sites on the island itself. The missiles could carry nuclear warheads and these could destroy cities within 2500 miles of Cuba. The photographs were taken by an American U2 spy plane.

1　It is 16 October 1962. You are one of President Kennedy's advisers and you have been shown Sources A–D on these pages. Produce a report for the president. Use the following headings in your report and find evidence to go underneath each one.

(a) Growing friendship between the USSR and Cuba
Use Source B for this and mention the growth in trade between the two.

(b) The danger Cuba is causing the USA
Mention missile sites and missiles, and ships carrying weapons towards Cuba.

(c) Suggested courses of action for the USA
Write down and comment on each of the following suggestions, all of which were actually made at the time by Kennedy's closest advisers.
i　Bomb Cuba.
ii　Impose a blockade on Cuba stopping all ships carrying weapons from going through.
iii　Do nothing.
iv　Bomb the USSR.

Source C　*A Russian ship heading towards Cuba*

Source D *Missile sites on the island of Cuba*

What really happened?

On 22 October 1962 Kennedy said the following on American television:

'All ships of any kind bound for Cuba from whatever nation or port will, if found to contain cargoes of offensive weapons, be turned back. It shall be the policy of this nation to regard any nuclear missile launched from Cuba against any nation in the Western hemisphere as an attack by the Soviet Union on the United States, requiring a full retaliatory response upon the Soviet Union. We will call for the dismantling of all offensive weapons in Cuba'.

Source E

2 a **What did Kennedy say he would do if a missile was launched from Cuba?**
   b **What would you have advised Khrushchev to do at this stage? Bomb the USA? Carry on sending weapons to Cuba? Do as Kennedy demanded? Give a reason for your answer.**

The following day a Russian ship, the *Bucharest*, was stopped and searched by US ships. It carried no weapons so it was allowed to continue to Cuba. The other Russian ships were ordered by Khrushchev to slow down. Kennedy threatened 'further action' unless the missile sites on Cuba were dismantled. It seemed as if Kennedy was prepared to risk war. The world waited nervously to see what Khrushchev would do.

Khrushchev said that *he* would remove all the missile sites from Cuba if the USA would remove all their missile sites from Turkey. Kennedy agreed in secret that this would be done and so Khrushchev backed down. The missile sites on Cuba were taken away and a war between the two superpowers had been avoided.

3 a **Describe how Khrushchev tried to see whether Kennedy really would search Russian ships for weapons.**
   b **What did Khrushchev demand should happen before the missile sites on Cuba were dismantled? Do you think he had a right to make such a demand or not? Say why.**

Some results of the crisis

Neither side wanted to come so close to war again. In 1963 the 'Hot Line' was set up between the USA and the USSR. This is a direct telephone link between the two leaders so that either leader can pick up a telephone and talk straight away to the other one if there is a crisis that might lead to war. In 1965 the USA, the USSR and Britain signed the Test Ban Treaty in which they all promised not to test nuclear weapons in the atmosphere. This was really the start of a policy that became known as *detente*. It means that the superpowers will try to solve their problems by talking to each other rather than by going to war.

Since 1963 the USA and the USSR have also had a number of SALT talks. SALT stands for Strategic Arms-Limitations Talks and they are attempts by the two superpowers to cut down the number of weapons they each have. The talks were set up because some people believe that the more weapons a country has then the more likely it is to go to war.

4 **Write down three things that were a result of the Cuba Crisis and give details of each.**

5 **Here is a list of dates on which events connected with the Cuba Crisis occurred. Look back over the chapter and then write down each date along with the event that happened on that day (the first one has been done for you).**

1959 Fidel Castro came to power in Cuba.
1961
16 October 1962
22 October 1962
23 October 1962

14 The Vietnam War

Source A   *A victim of a napalm bomb attack in Vietnam*

Imagine if, instead of waking up in the morning and eating your cornflakes, the first thing you saw when you opened your eyes was daylight because your house had been destroyed. This is what happened to the girl in Source A. She was also very badly burnt from the effects of a bomb that American helicopters had dropped on her village. The bomb contained a chemical called napalm that caused widespread fire. What is really strange about all this is that the Americans were using techniques such as this in South Vietnam (see Source C) because they said they wanted to *help* the people in the villages they were destroying. They were forcing these people to move out of their villages to special camps so that American soldiers could set up special 'hamlets' in their place, from which they could attack Communists coming in from North Vietnam. How did such an awful situation ever come about? Look carefully at the time chart below and answer the questions which follow it and you might understand a little more.

Source B   *The war in Vietnam*

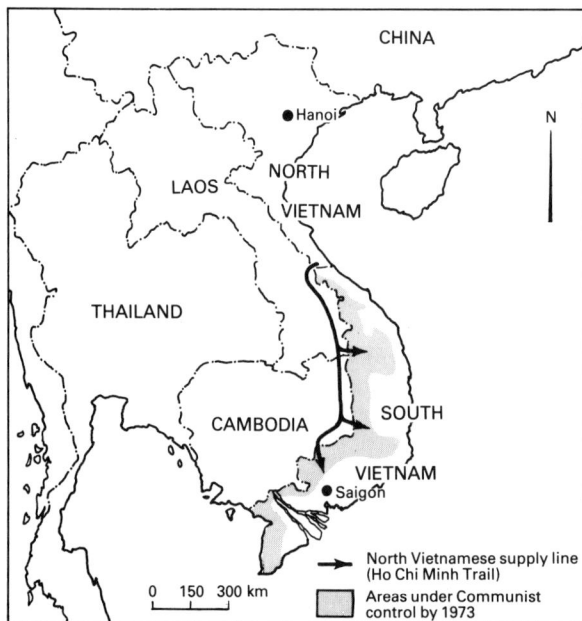

Time chart of main events in the Vietnam War

Pre 1945	Vietnam controlled by France
1954	Battle of Dien Bien Phu. French lost war against Vietnam.
1955	Geneva peace conference set up North and South Vietnam as separate countries. The North was Communist and ruled by Ho Chi Minh. The South was left free to decide its own fate.
1955–60	The USA sent arms and millions of dollars to South Vietnam because they did not want the Communist North Vietnamese to take over. If this happened the USA feared that the Communists might also take over Laos and Cambodia. (See Source B.)
1960–63	Ho Chi Minh sent help to the rebels of South Vietnam to help them overthrow their government. These rebels became known as the *Vietcong*.
1964	US ships patrolled the coast of Vietnam to stop the North from supplying the rebels by sea. In August the North Vietnamese attacked an American destroyer in the Gulf of Tonking.
1964–65	The USA carried out intensive bombing of North Vietnam in order to destroy bridges and supply lines. One-and-a-half million US troops were sent to fight in Vietnam. The USSR supplied aid and weapons to Ho Chi Minh in the North. Lots of supplies were smuggled from North to South Vietnam on bicycles through secret tracks in the forests known as *The Ho Chi Minh Trail*.
1968 (a)	The Communists of the North almost broke through to the South in the Tet Offensive.
(b)	Millions of Americans were horrified by television pictures (like Source A) shown at home. They began to protest and the war became unpopular in America.
1969	President Nixon of the USA began 'Vietnamisation', which meant that he wanted US troops to move out and give supplies to the South Vietnamese so that they could fight their own war.
1973	A ceasefire was agreed at Paris. The Americans went home.

| 1975 | South Vietnam surrendered to the North and became ruled by Communists. Cambodia was also taken over by the Communist Khmer Rouge army. |

1 **Finish the following sentences by looking at the information in the time chart.**

1 The _____ ruled Vietnam until 1954 when they were beaten at the battle of ____ ____ ___.
2 The USA sent help to South Vietnam because ... (Complete the sentence.)
3 Ho Chi Minh was the leader of ____ Vietnam.
4 The ____ supplied weapons to Ho Chi Minh in the North and these were smuggled south along the __ __ ____ trail.
5 The war became unpopular in the USA because ... (Complete the sentence.)
6 When the Americans went home in 1973 the war was later won by ____.

The horrors of the war

Source A shows the results of one of the horrors of the war, the use of napalm by the USA. Source C shows the results of a chemical used to defoliate, or get rid of plant life. The Americans did this so that the Vietcong would not be able to hide in the forests and attack their soldiers. In 1967 Ho Chi Minh described what *he* thought about the American presence in Vietnam:

'Vietnam is thousands of miles away from the United States. The Vietnamese people have never done any harm to the US ... Half a million US troops have resorted to the most inhuman weapons and the most barbarous methods of warfare, such as napalm, toxic chemicals and gases, to massacre our compatriots, destroy crops and rase villages to the ground. In North Vietnam thousands of US aircraft have dropped thousands of bombs destroying towns, villages and factories, roads, bridges, dykes, dams and even churches, hospitals and schools.'

Source D

President Johnson of the USA, however, felt that America had every right to do these things because, he said:

'Most of the non communist nations of Asia cannot, by themselves and alone, resist the growing might and grasping ambition of Asian communism. Our power, therefore, is a vital shield. If we are driven from the field in Vietnam then no nation can ever again have the same confidence in American promises or American protection ... An Asia so threatened by communist domination would imperil the security of the United States itself.'

Source E

Source C *The effect of defoliation. This area was thick forest before it was defoliated by the Americans*

2 What sort of techniques did the USA use to try to win the war in Vietnam? Describe them and say in each case whether or not you think she had the right to do these things.

3 a Explain in your own words the reason that President Johnson gave for the USA taking part in the Vietnam War.
  b Remember the Domino Theory? (See Chapter 6.) In what ways could the US presence in Vietnam be connected with this theory?

33

15 Conflict in the Middle East

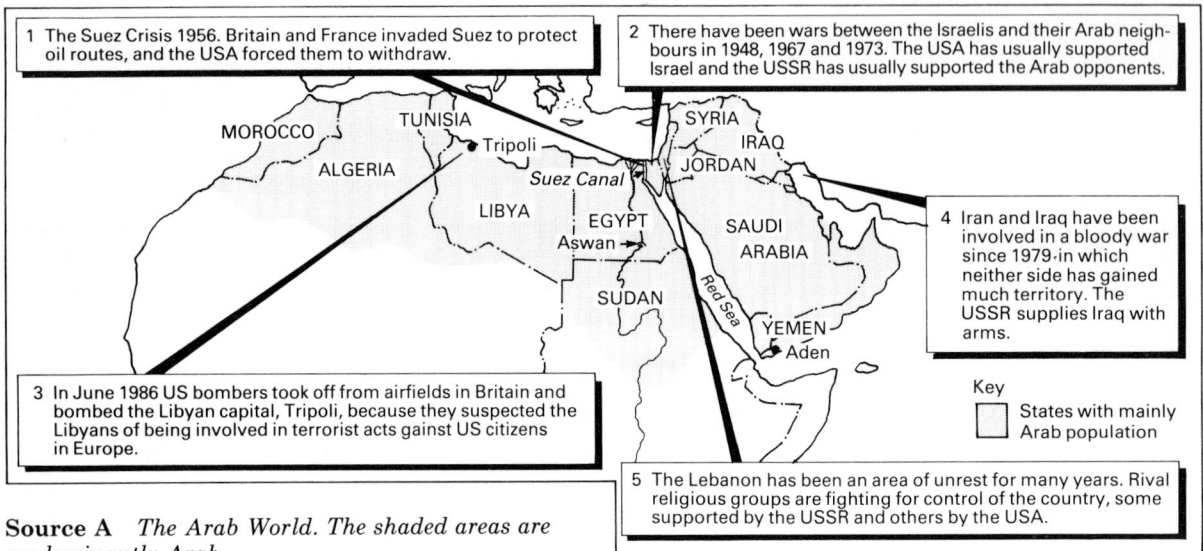

1 The Suez Crisis 1956. Britain and France invaded Suez to protect oil routes, and the USA forced them to withdraw.

2 There have been wars between the Israelis and their Arab neighbours in 1948, 1967 and 1973. The USA has usually supported Israel and the USSR has usually supported the Arab opponents.

4 Iran and Iraq have been involved in a bloody war since 1979 in which neither side has gained much territory. The USSR supplies Iraq with arms.

3 In June 1986 US bombers took off from airfields in Britain and bombed the Libyan capital, Tripoli, because they suspected the Libyans of being involved in terrorist acts gainst US citizens in Europe.

Key

☐ States with mainly Arab population

5 The Lebanon has been an area of unrest for many years. Rival religious groups are fighting for control of the country, some supported by the USSR and others by the USA.

Source A *The Arab World. The shaded areas are predominantly Arab*

Source A shows five main problems that have arisen in the Middle East since the end of the Second World War. The USA and USSR have been involved in these events by giving support to one side or the other.

1 **Use Sources A and B to fill out and complete a chart like the one below. Use ticks to show which country supported each event.**

Event	USA supported	USSR supported
1 Suez crisis 1956		
2 Arab-Israeli wars since 1949		
3 Libyan support of terrorist groups in the Middle East		
4 The Gulf War between Iran and Iraq		
5 The fighting in the Lebanon between rival religious groups		

How and why did the superpowers get involved?

The USA and the USSR cooperated with the United Nations organisation to set up the state of Israel in 1948. But when Britain withdrew from the area the two superpowers tried to gain influence there. The USA actually sent money and arms to Turkey, Iran and Iraq (Arab nations) while the USSR gave financial help and aid to Egypt and Syria. But the Arab nations never

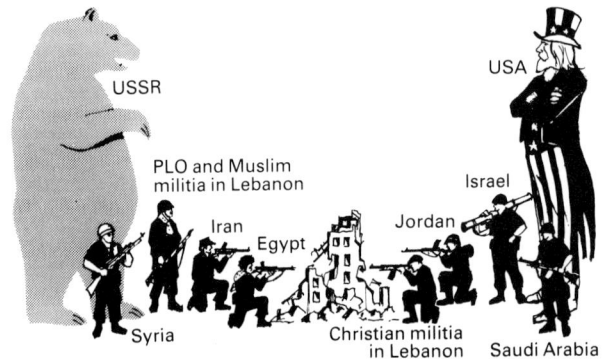

Source B *Superpower involvement in the Middle East*

really wanted an American *or* Soviet influence. They only used their money because they needed it. But a real crisis occurred in 1956 in Egypt.

The Suez Crisis, 1956

In 1956 Nasser, the leader of Egypt, borrowed money from the USA to build the Aswan Dam in Egypt. But at the same time Khrushchev, the leader of the USSR, was supplying Egypt with weapons to help them against Israel. Nasser did not want to be too heavily influenced by either side and so he also asked Mao Zedong (the leader of China) for help.

All this angered the USA and she took away her money for the new dam. Khrushchev said that *he* would help the Egyptians to build the dam. This worried Britain, as Soviet influence in Egypt might threaten the route used by British ships carrying oil from the area. (See Source A.)

When Israeli forces attacked the Egyptians on 29 October 1956, British and French troops landed along the Suez Canal to protect the oil routes. The USA forced the British and French troops to withdraw because she was annoyed that Britain and France had taken action without asking her first. This left the USA supporting Israel and the USSR supporting Egypt. The two major superpowers seemed to be in conflict again. There have been Arab/Israeli wars in 1967 and again in 1973 and on both occasions the USA has supported Israel and the USSR has supported Egypt.

The major reason why the USA is so heavily involved in Middle Eastern affairs is because she buys much of her oil from that area and so she wants to make sure she can stop wars from breaking out there. But the USA has done more than support one side. She has also made genuine efforts to get a peace settlement between Israel and her Arab neighbours, as you will see in the next section.

---

2   **Which countries (or leaders of countries) do you think might have said each of the statements below. Write out the name of the country and then the statement next to it.**

Statements

1   'I will borrow money from the USA to build the Aswan Dam but I will also get arms from the USSR to help my country fight the Israelis'.
2   'If Nasser approaches China and Russia for help, we will withdraw our offer of money to build the dam'.
3   'We must land our troops along the Suez Canal to protect the oil routes'.
4   'You should have asked us first if you could land troops along the Suez Canal. We demand that you take them away'.

The Americans' attempt at a peace solution

In 1973 a conference chaired by both the USA and the USSR met for only two days before elections in Israel prevented it continuing. Henry Kissinger of the USA flew thousands of miles to talk to the leaders of Syria, Egypt and Israel between 1973 and 1976 but he never managed to reach a solution. The basic problem is that both the Arabs *and* the Israelis claim that they have a right to live in Palestine and neither side has been willing

to give in or accept that the others have any right at all to be there.

In March 1979 a peace treaty between Israel and Egypt was signed in Washington after 'The Camp David Agreement' reached largely through the efforts of President Carter of the USA. A further US peace plan was put forward by President Reagan of the USA in 1982 in which all sides in the dispute agreed some concessions to the others. There is not space in this book to give the details of all these attempts. But these examples show that superpower involvement in the Middle East has been not entirely a destructive one.

Nevertheless, superpower conflict anywhere is obviously very dangerous and in 1986 the USA took direct military action in the Middle East and North Africa.

The USA attack on Libya, June 1986

The photograph, Source C, shows the remains of a discotheque in Berlin after terrorists had planted a bomb there. The discotheque was popular with US servicemen stationed in Germany and the USA claimed that she had evidence that the bomb attack had been planned by terrorists supported by Colonel Gadaffi, the leader of Libya. As a result, Margaret Thatcher, the British prime minister, gave her permission for American war planes to set off from bases in Britain. The planes flew around France because the French government refused to allow them through their airspace. The planes bombed the centre of Tripoli, the capital of Libya, as a warning to the Libyans not to attack Americans in Europe again.

---

3   a   **Try to make two lists, one about the ways the USA has tried to help solve problems in the Middle East and another about the ways she might have made things worse.**
    b   **Do you think the USA had a right to bomb Libya in 1986 or not? Say why.**

Source C   *A Berlin discotheque bombed by terrorists in 1986*

16 Superpower rivalry in Africa

The superpowers are involved in so many parts of Africa that it is not possible to describe in detail in a short book like this one all that they do. We will concentrate therefore mainly on their involvement in Angola as an example. But it *is* possible to get a picture of their involvement in the continent by drawing a simple map (see question 1).

1 Use Source A and an atlas or ask your teacher for an outline map of Africa with the outlines of the countries marked on. Copy the information from Source A onto your own map.
   a Mark with an X the areas of armed conflict between the superpowers, that is Ethiopia, Chad, Western Sahara, Angola, Namibia, Mozambique.
   b Shade red the countries that the USSR supply with aid and arms, that is Mali, Algeria, Libya, Ethiopia, Guinea, Liberia, Benin, Congo, Angola, Uganda, Tanzania, Mozambique, Malagasy Republic.
   c Put stripes across the countries to which the USA supply arms, that is Morocco, Egypt, Liberia, Ghana, Nigeria, Ethiopia, Zaire, Kenya.
   d Put a key onto your map showing what the shading and symbols you have used stand for. Call your map 'Superpower involvement in Africa'.

2 One of the main reasons why the USA wants to gain influence over the countries around the coast of Africa is shown in Source A. What do you think the reason is?

Why did the superpowers become involved in Africa?

Your answer to question 2 should have taught you that one reason the superpowers are interested in the coastal countries of Africa is so that they can protect the routes of tankers delivering oil from the Persian Gulf. But there are other reasons why they got involved in Africa.

After 1945 countries such as Britain and France began to give independence to countries in Africa that they had once ruled over. One of the biggest problems the newly independent countries faced was how to develop their economies in order to raise the standard of living of their people. You saw in the previous chapter how Egypt tried to

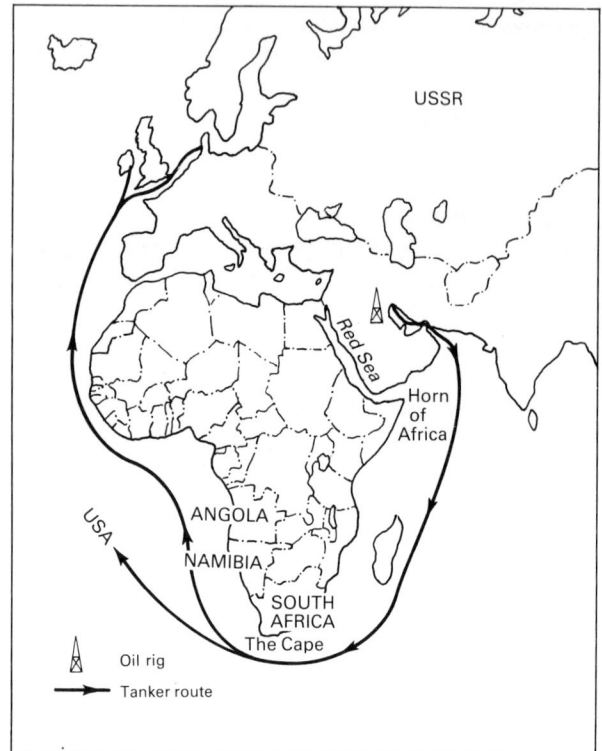

Source A   *Oil trading routes around Africa*

use both American *and* Russian money to build a dam. She was trying to play off one superpower against another without allowing either of them to gain too much influence in Egypt. Many other African countries tried to do the same thing. Most of them were less successful than Egypt at keeping the superpowers out.

After the Second World War the USA saw Africa as a golden opportunity for exporting to and trading with. They saw that they could make a lot of money out of trading with African countries. The USA, for instance, buys 47 per cent of Nigeria's oil and sells goods worth 1000 million dollars a year to Nigeria itself. The map that you drew for question 1 will show you the other countries to which the USA supplies arms.

The USSR on the other hand also supplies aid to many African countries. *Her* main reason is that she wants to spread the idea of Communism and help fight off Western influence in Africa. It is almost as if neither the USA nor the USSR really know what they stand to gain from Africa but they are both afraid of letting the other side get the upper hand in any part of the world.

3 Draw out a chart using the headings below and write three points in each section of it.

Reasons for USA involvement in Africa	Reasons for USSR involvement in Africa

Angola: an example of superpower rivalry in Africa

Perhaps the best example of the result of USA and USSR involvement in Africa is their role in Angola (see Source A). Source B shows a young boy fighting for the MPLA in Angola. 'MPLA' stands for the Popular Front for the Liberation of Angola and its main rivals are the UNITA (Total Independence for Angola) forces. How old do you think the boy is? Do you think he really understands what he is fighting for? He fights because the people of Angola have been involved in a bloody civil war since 1975.

In 1974 the Portuguese withdrew from Angola. They had ruled it for 400 years but could no longer fight off the rebel forces that were fighting for their independence. These rebel forces were the MPLA, UNITA and the FNLA (National Front for the Liberation of Angola). When the Portuguese moved out, these groups fought amongst themselves. The Russians saw this as an opportunity to gain influence over a coastal African state from which they could threaten the West's oil routes (see Source A). But the Russians were reluctant to send troops into Africa at a time when relations with the West were poor in case they were accused of wanting to provoke a world war. They got Cuba to help instead. Cuban soldiers helped the MPLA who quickly defeated the others and set up a government in Angola in 1975.

But by 1980 this government was being challenged. SWAPO (South West African People's Organisation) guerrillas were attacking from Namibia (see Source C). UNITA reappeared and with help from South Africa they have even penetrated into the northern parts of Angola. In 1987 at the time this book was being written, the war in Angola was still going on.

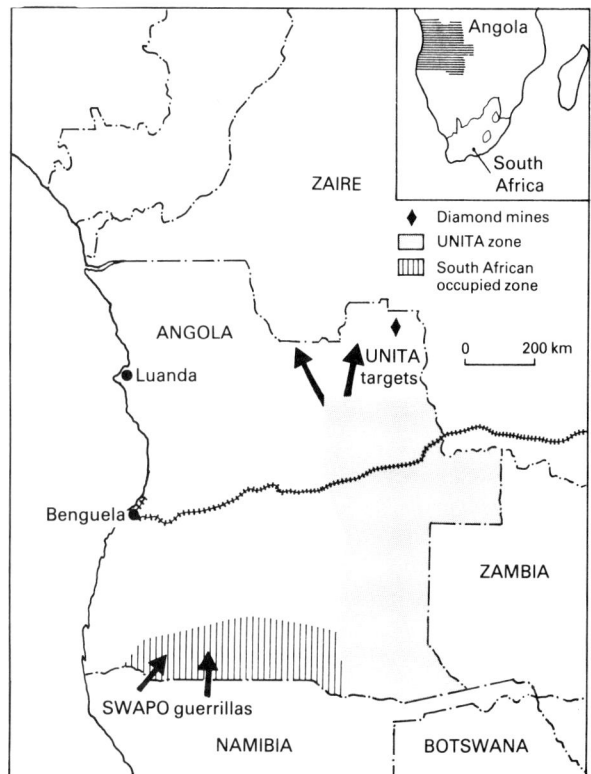

Source C *The war in Angola*

Source B *An MPLA boy soldier*

4 Imagine you are fighting in one of the armies that have been involved in the war in Angola. Explain why you are fighting and what you hope to achieve. You will need to mention which side is supporting you (the USA supported UNITA) and why you are fighting for one side and not the other. Describe the main events of the war as if you had actually fought in them.

17 Keeping up with 'the Joneses': other rivalries

You have seen throughout this book that whenever one of the superpowers, either the USA or the USSR, gets involved in something then the other one seems to follow. (China has very much kept apart but her role will be looked at more closely in the next chapter.) The list seems almost endless: when the USSR got involved in Korea then so did the USA (see Chapter 9). The same was the case in Vietnam (Chapter 14), the Middle East (Chapter 15) and in Africa (Chapter 16). It seems as if each side will get involved in whatever the other one does just to make sure they do not miss out on an opportunity to prove that they are as strong as each other. In Britain, we call this 'keeping up with the Joneses'. It is supposed to mean that if you have neighbours (in this case called Jones) you try all the time to buy bigger and better things than they do just to show that you are as good as they are.

Perhaps the best example of non-political rivalry between the two main superpowers is in sport.

Rivalry in sport

Source A shows a Soviet and an American athlete competing on the running track. The picture really symbolises or sums up the idea of the two nations racing to prove to the rest of the world which one of them is the best. Source B shows the successes of the USA and the USSR in Olympic games.

Source A *Russian and US athletes competing at the Olympics*

Source B

Medal successes in Olympic games 1896–1980

	Gold	Silver	Bronze	Total
USA	660	511	444	1613
USSR	402	330	298	1028

Both countries make a great deal of fuss when their athletes do well in the Olympic games and Americans like nothing better than to beat Russians. The Russians feel the same about beating Americans. In 1980 the Russians built a magnificent stadium in Moscow when the Olympic games were held there. This was to impress the rest of the world as it watched on television. However, the USA brought their rivalry with Russia into sport. As a protest against Russia's invasion of Afghanistan, the USA refused to take part in the Moscow Olympics. In 1984, when the games were held in Los Angeles in the USA, the Russians refused to take part because they claimed they were not satisfied that their athletes would be safe when they were in America. This is yet another example of how these two superpowers never seem to miss an opportunity to let the rest of the world know how they feel about each other.

---

1 Why do both superpowers want to do well in competitions like the Olympic games? How do they think it will affect their standing with the rest of the world?

---

2 If you were an American athlete in 1980 or a Russian athlete in 1984, describe how you would feel about your country's decision not to take part in the Olympics. Write a sort of diary of your thoughts about it. (Don't forget, you might well agree with the reasons why they withdrew but still feel upset about not being able to take part.)

---

3 Some people said that when one of these countries did not take part it 'devalued the medals'. What do you think this means?

The space race

Another non-political way that the USA and the

USSR have tried to outdo each other is in their space exploration programmes. This became like a race to see who could make discoveries first, as you can see from this chart. Both nations poured vast amounts of money into their space programmes to show the rest of the world how good their technology was. Both sides have achieved a great deal but one wonders how much more they might have achieved if they had worked together on more projects instead of on their own.

The space race

USA	USSR
1957	*Sputnik I* the first satellite is launched.
1959	Russian spaceship photographs the far side of the moon.
1961	Yuri Gagarin becomes the first man in space and orbits the earth.
1962 John Glenn orbits the earth.	
1963	Valentina Tereschova becomes the first woman in space.
1964	The first three-man satellite is launched.
1968 Apollo 8 orbits the moon.	
1969 Neil Armstrong becomes the first man on the moon.	
1972 Apollo 16 photographs the mountains on the moon.	
1975 Joint Soyuz–Apollo mission and the handshake in space.	
1981 Space shuttle launched. The first reusable space craft.	

Source C *Planting the US flag on the moon*

4 Copy the table showing the space race.
  a Which country started the space race in your opinion, and in what way?
  b Which country got the first man on the moon?
  c What is meant by the term 'the space race' and do you think anyone has won it?
  d Do you think the space race improves or worsens relations between the USA and the USSR? Explain your answer.

Spies

Both the USA and the USSR spy on each other constantly to see if they can find out what the other country is up to. The whole world knows this happens. Yet occasionally, for some reason or another, one or other of these superpowers decides to make a big issue out of it. Source D shows Nicholas Daniloff, an American journalist working in Russia, and Zakharov, a Russian embassy official working in America. In September 1986 Daniloff was arrested in Russia and accused of spying for the USA. He denied the charge. In retaliation the USA arrested Zakharov and accused *him* of spying for the USSR. The Americans used the Daniloff case as an excuse to threaten to call off a special summit meeting on defence which was to take place later that year between the two leaders, president Reagan of the USA and premier Gorbachev of the USSR.

Source D *Daniloff (left) and Zakharov (right)*

3 Think of two reasons why you might consider that spying is all right and two reasons why you might say it is wrong.

18 China and the superpowers since 1949

You have probably noticed that China has not appeared as much as the USA and the USSR throughout this book. From 1949 onwards China was a Communist country. Her relations with the other superpowers and with the rest of the world have ranged from friendship to outright hostility.

China's relationship with the USSR

Source A shows that relations between the USSR and China started off on a friendly basis in 1949 when she signed an aid treaty. The USSR promised money and advisers to China to help China rebuild the factories and industries that had been destroyed during the civil war that brought Mao Zedong and the Communist party to power. But during the 1950s the two countries began to disagree over which should be the leader of the Communist world. The Chinese accused the USSR of becoming too much like the capitalist Western powers. China claimed that Chinese Communism was much more like what true Communism should be.

The USSR refused to share her secrets on atomic bombs with China and in 1960 she stopped sending aid to China and withdrew her advisers. Relations were at their worst by 1969 when China exploded her first atomic bomb, proving she could be a real threat as a world power, and Russian troops were killed by Chinese soldiers in a border incident.

China has had disputes over her border with the USSR and India since 1949, and it was fighting over one of these areas that caused the deaths in 1969.

Source A *Soviet/Chinese relations since 1949*

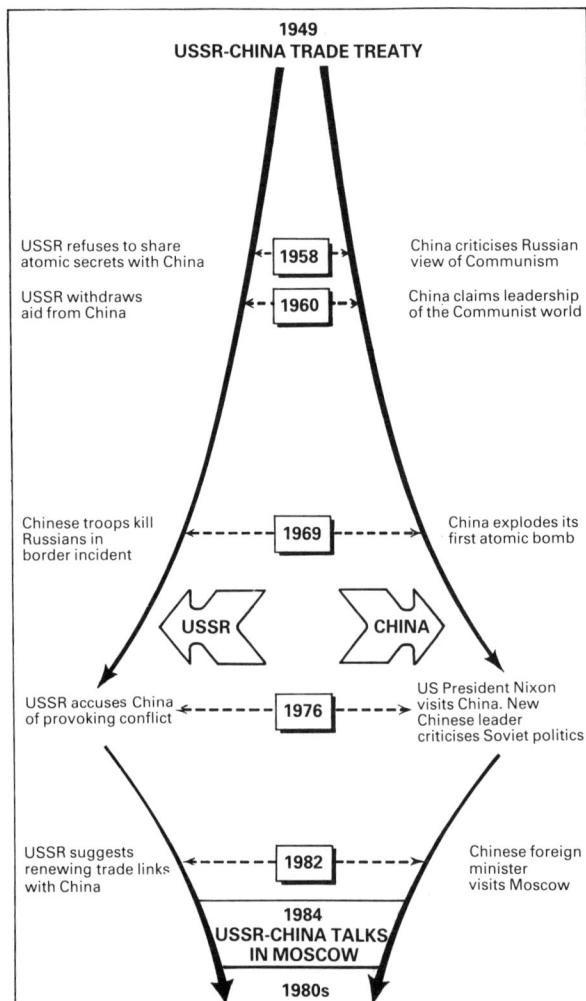

1949
USSR-CHINA TRADE TREATY

USSR refuses to share atomic secrets with China	1958	China criticises Russian view of Communism
USSR withdraws aid from China	1960	China claims leadership of the Communist world
Chinese troops kill Russians in border incident	1969	China explodes its first atomic bomb

USSR ◄ CHINA ►

USSR accuses China of provoking conflict	1976	US President Nixon visits China. New Chinese leader criticises Soviet politics
USSR suggests renewing trade links with China	1982	Chinese foreign minister visits Moscow

1984
USSR-CHINA TALKS IN MOSCOW

1980s

1 **Look at Source A. Which of the statements below might have been said by a Russian leader and which by a Chinese? Explain how you reached your decision.**

Statements
1 'We refuse to share our atomic secrets with you until you recognise our right to be leaders of the Communist world.'
2 'If you do not like the way we practice Communism, we will withdraw all our aid from your country.'
3 'You have provoked us by killing our soldiers along your border and by trying to threaten us by exploding an atomic bomb.'
4 'We will show how independent we are by inviting the president of the USA to visit our country.'
5 'We wish to show our willingness to be friendly by sending our foreign minister to visit Moscow.'
6 'We would like to begin trading with your country again.'

2 **At what stage between 1949 and 1984 would you say that relations between China and the USSR were at their worst? Explain your answer.**

During the 1980s relationships between China and the USSR have been much friendlier. The USSR feels that she needs China as a friend; they feel surrounded and threatened by the NATO countries. Also, the USSR has had to keep half-a-million troops stationed along the border with China. This is proving to be expensive. China has welcomed the friendlier relations but she still criticises the USSR at times, for example when Russian troops invaded Afghanistan in 1980. So China seems willing to be friendlier but not willing to be dominated by the USSR.

China and the USA

Source B shows a map by Chu Yu-lien who was Chinese Foreign minister during the 1960s. It is meant to show his view of US imperialism, or desire to take over other countries in South East Asia, during the 1960s.

---

3 a What two words or phrases in Source B strongly suggest that its writer is anti-American?

b What three pictures or symbols are used to show that this writer thinks the USA is aggressive.

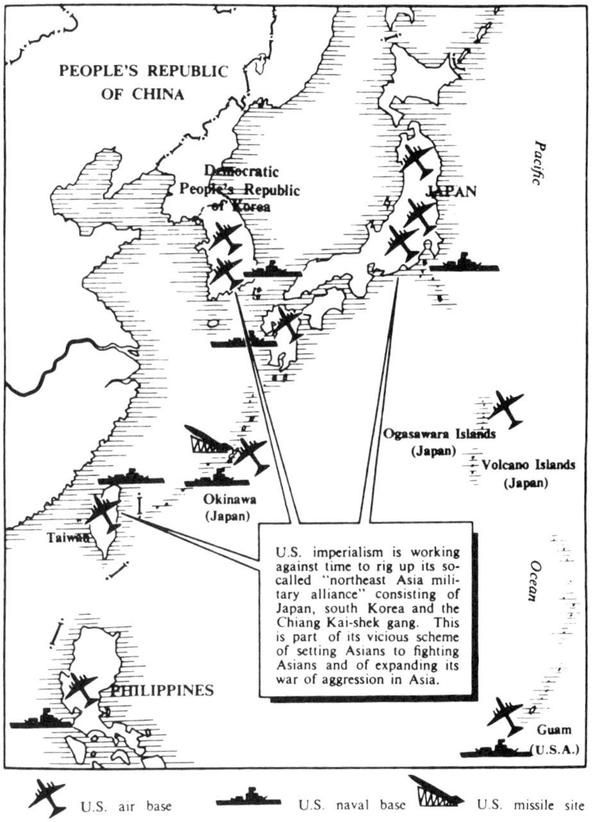
PEOPLE'S REPUBLIC OF CHINA
Democratic People's Republic of Korea
JAPAN
Pacific
Ocean
Ogasawara Islands (Japan)
Volcano Islands (Japan)
Okinawa (Japan)
Taiwan
PHILIPPINES
Guam (U.S.A.)
U.S. imperialism is working against time to rig up its so-called "northeast Asia military alliance" consisting of Japan, south Korea and the Chiang Kai-shek gang. This is part of its vicious scheme of setting Asians to fighting Asians and of expanding its war of aggression in Asia.
U.S. air base
U.S. naval base
U.S. missile site

Source B *Sketch of US disposition for aggression in North-East Asia*

Source B shows that the Chinese were no more friendly towards the USA during the 1960s than they were towards the USSR. They were trying to be the truly independent superpower.

Relations between China and the West began to improve after 1971 when China was admitted to the United Nations. In 1976 Mao Zedong, the Chinese leader, died. The new leaders felt that a long period of peace was needed for China to modernise her industries. This attitude helped lead to friendlier relations with the West. The USA also wanted friendship with China, to try to prevent an alliance between China and the USSR.

In 1971 an American table tennis team was invited to visit China and in 1972 President Nixon of the USA visited China. Full diplomatic relations between the two countries were opened in 1979 and the new Chinese leader, Deng Xiaoping, visited President Carter in Washington.

Since that time American firms have been almost falling over themselves to sell their products in China. For example, in 1983 Texaco and Chevron began drilling for oil in Chinese waters. By 1984 there were more than 120 American firms based in Peking. In 1984 the USA agreed to sell missiles to China. The Chinese believe that trade with the USA will help them to modernise their country and make them safer against other superpowers.

But the new friendly relationship between the USA and China could also be a threat to world peace. The Chinese distrust the USSR even more than the USA does. China has frequently told the USA not to reduce her arms and not to enter arms reduction talks with the USSR. Many people believe that it could be China, with a quarter of the world's population, that could bring about war between the superpowers rather than the USA or the USSR.

---

4 a Why did China want to improve relations with the USA?

b Why do you think these relations have been called 'ping pong diplomacy' since they first started in 1971?

c In what way might the relations between the USA and China prove to be a danger to world peace?

Some people believe that the Cold War will cause a third World War started by the USA and the USSR. Source A shows the strength of both countries' forces and top military experts' views about how such a war might begin if the USSR attack.

---

1 a If there was a traditional war in Europe between the USA and the USSR (that is a war where nuclear weapons were not used) who do you think would be most likely to win? Say why.

b Try to explain in a short paragraph the four stages of attack shown in the map in Source A.

c This map assumes that the USSR will attack first. What do you think the order of attack might be if the NATO forces attacked the USSR?

Everyone in the world fears the possible effects of a nuclear war. In 1945 the only nuclear bombs to be dropped were released from American aeroplanes on the Japanese cities of Hiroshima and Nagasaki. In Hiroshima everyone within two miles of where the bomb fell was killed and all buildings were destroyed by the heat and fire that was caused. Up to five miles away buildings were destroyed by a blast of hot air travelling at 500 miles an hour. For months afterwards people who wore spectacles were removing fagments of shattered glass from their eyes. In the outskirts of the city some people saw thousands of people running away from the blast and thought they were Negroes because their skin had been blackened by heat. For years afterwards people died from radiation caused by the bomb and even babies born years later were affected.

The nuclear bombs that the superpowers now possess are more than a thousand times more powerful than the Hiroshima bomb of 1945. Source B shows the probable effects of just one of these bombs landing on central London.

---

2 Using Source B say what would happen to each of the following if a nuclear bomb fell on London.

a The Houses of Parliament (Area A).

b Spectators in the stands at Epsom race course.

c People shopping in Welwyn Garden City.

d People waving goodbye to friends at Luton airport.

e Dockers working on the dockside at Portsmouth.

---

3 Find a map of your own area and write down what the effects would be if a nuclear bomb fell on your nearest town or city.

Source A   *The balance of forces between the superpowers*

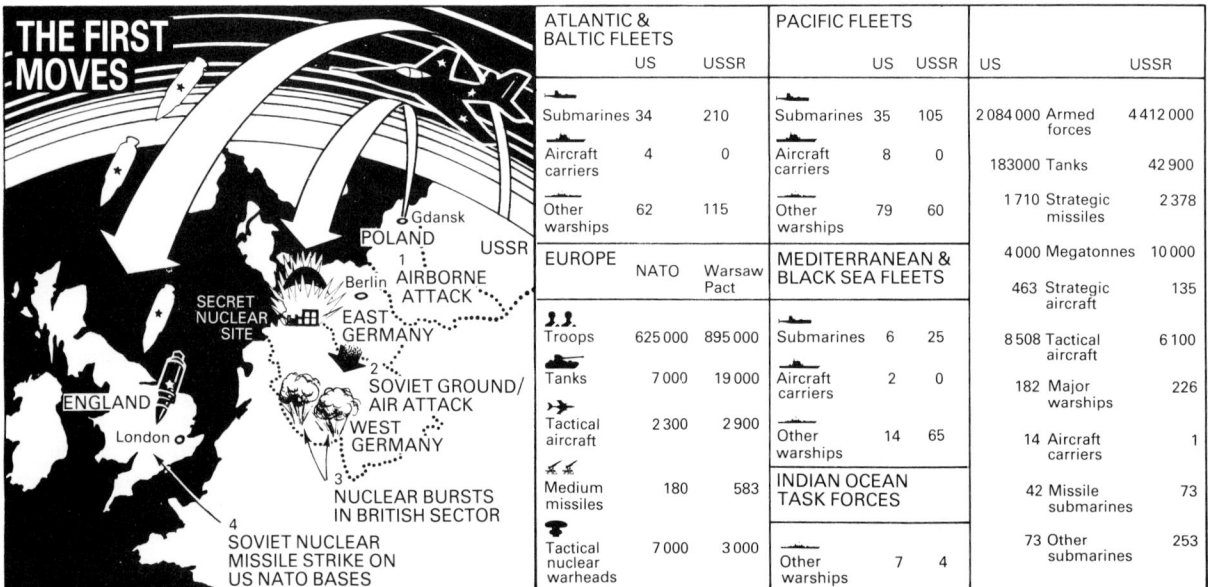

THE FIRST MOVES

Map labels: Gdansk; POLAND; USSR; Berlin; 1 AIRBORNE ATTACK; EAST GERMANY; SECRET NUCLEAR SITE; 2 SOVIET GROUND/AIR ATTACK; ENGLAND; London; WEST GERMANY; 3 NUCLEAR BURSTS IN BRITISH SECTOR; 4 SOVIET NUCLEAR MISSILE STRIKE ON US NATO BASES

ATLANTIC & BALTIC FLEETS		
	US	USSR
Submarines	34	210
Aircraft carriers	4	0
Other warships	62	115

EUROPE	NATO	Warsaw Pact
Troops	625 000	895 000
Tanks	7 000	19 000
Tactical aircraft	2 300	2 900
Medium missiles	180	583
Tactical nuclear warheads	7 000	3 000

PACIFIC FLEETS		
	US	USSR
Submarines	35	105
Aircraft carriers	8	0
Other warships	79	60

MEDITERRANEAN & BLACK SEA FLEETS	US	USSR
Submarines	6	25
Aircraft carriers	2	0
Other warships	14	65

INDIAN OCEAN TASK FORCES	US	USSR
Other warships	7	4

	US		USSR
	2 084 000	Armed forces	4 412 000
	183 000	Tanks	42 900
	1 710	Strategic missiles	2 378
	4 000	Megatonnes	10 000
	463	Strategic aircraft	135
	8 508	Tactical aircraft	6 100
	182	Major warships	226
	14	Aircraft carriers	1
	42	Missile submarines	73
	73	Other submarines	253

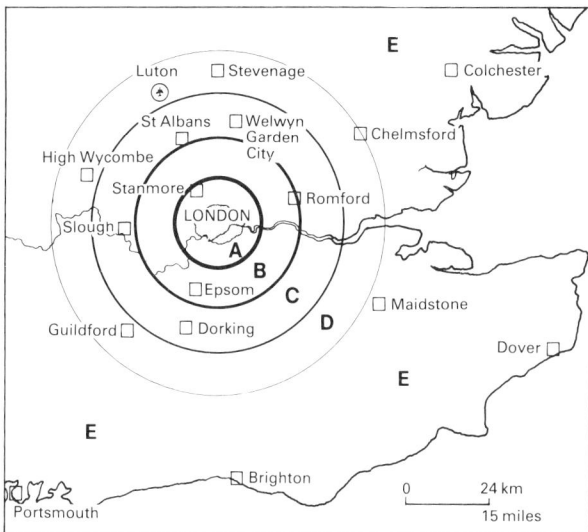

AREA A (up to 7½ miles, 12 kilometres, from the centre). Temperatures reach 10 million degrees centigrade. Complete destruction of all buildings and life immediately.
AREA B (up to 15 miles, 24 kilometres, from the centre). Rubber and plastic burst into flames. Buses would simply melt around their passengers and aircraft at Heathrow airport would explode. A very high death toll.
AREA C (up to 22½ miles, 36 kilometes, away from the centre). Unpainted woodwork would burst into flames. Extensive damage to many buildings due to shock waves. Thousands of people would suffer severe burns and doses of radiation.
AREA D (up to 30 miles, 50 kilometres, from the centre). Less damage to buildings but water and electricity supplies would be cut. People out in the open would be burnt as their clothes would catch fire.
AREA E (more than 30 miles, 50 milometres, from the centre). People will still be severely burned and might take years to die from radiation sickness. People on the beach at Brighton in the middle of winter would get an immediate tan.

Source B *The effects of a single nuclear bomb landing on the Houses of Parliament in London*

Look at Source C. It shows what the British government think you should do to keep safe after a nuclear attack. The pamphlet, 'Protect And Survive', also says that you should make sure you take the following into your shelter: 3½ gallons of drinking water per person; tinned food; portable radio; warm clothing; blankets and plastic bags; clock; toys and magazines and so on.

4   **Here are four comments made by famous people about nuclear weapons. Put the one you agree with most at the top of your list and the one you disagree with at the bottom. Say why you put your first one first and your last one last.**

1   The Church And The Bomb, 1962
'Even a small first use of nuclear weapons would never be morally justified in view of the high risk that this would lead to full scale nuclear warfare.'
2   Casper Wienberger, US Defence Secretary
'Our goal is a freeze on the building of all nuclear weapons from now onwards, followed by a gradual reduction in the numbers of weapons held by each side.'
3   General Arnold, Chief of USA air staff 1945
'Real security . . . in the visible future will rest on our ability to take immediate offensive action with overwhelming force.
4   David Owen, SDP MP in 1980
'Britain has been at peace for 35 years. The harsh reality behind that peace has been the fact that every political leader throughout that period has known that starting a major war brings the risk of massive nuclear retaliation.'

Source C *These pictures are from a British Government pamphlet "Protect and Survive" (now out of print). They show how people can build shelters to protect themselves from fall-out from a nuclear attack. These shelters would not protect people from the blast of a nuclear bomb.*

20 Attempts to maintain peace

There have been lots of examples throughout this book of how relations between the superpowers have been tense or have almost led to war. But it must not be forgotten that the superpowers have also made great efforts to avoid war and to improve relations. All sides realise the dangers of conventional and nuclear war and they try very hard to make sure that such events never happen. One of the ways they do this is by working through the United Nations (see Chapter 1). Another method is by arranging meetings between the leaders of the countries to talk about problems between them. There are some examples of such meetings shown in the photographs on the next page. World leaders often think that they can avoid conflicts if they meet each other, get to know each other and perhaps therefore learn to trust one another.

But it is on the issue of arms control that the superpowers have concentrated the most. On these two pages you can read about ten attempts since 1963 to limit or control various kinds of weapons including nuclear weapons.

Although the list of arms talks looks impressive, it is worth noting that the USA and the USSR are continuing to build up their stores of nuclear weapons. The INF and START talks broke down because the USSR complained about the fact that NATO was putting cruise missiles into Europe while the talks were actually going on. In 1986 arms reduction talks between the USA and the USSR broke down because the USA refused to stop developing a system known as 'Star Wars' designed to destroy nuclear missiles from outer space. (See Chapter 21.)

---

1 Read the attempts at arms control in boxes 1–9 and then complete a chart using the headings below. The last column should be for your own thoughts and comments about how useful you think the attempt was or what problems you can foresee because of it.

Year	Title of treaty	Countries involved	Main things decided	Your own comment

---

1 *1963, the Partial Test Ban Treaty*
Britain, the USA and the USSR agreed to stop testing nuclear weapons in the atmosphere. Tests would only be carried out underground.

2 *1967, Outer Space Treaty*
60 countries agreed not to send nuclear weapons into space.

3 *1968, the Nuclear Non-Proliferation Treaty*
90 countries agreed not to exchange knowledge about nuclear weapons in the hope that this would limit the number that were developed.

4 *1971, the Seabed Pact*
40 countries agreed not to place nuclear weapons on the seabed within 20 kilometres of another country's limits.

5 *1972, Biological Warfare Treaty*
30 countries banned the storage and use of biological weapons and demanded the destruction of those that already existed.

9 *1982 START (Strategic Arms Reduction Talks)*
Geneva talks again; this time to reduce the number of long-range nuclear missiles held by the superpowers.

8 *1961, INF (Intermediate-range Nuclear Forces) talks*
Talks began in Geneva to limit the number of nuclear arms positioned in Europe.

7 *1979, SALT 2*
New limits were put on the number of nuclear weapons to be held by the USA and the USSR.

6 *1972, Strategic Arms Limitation Talks (SALT) 1*
This was the first agreement between the USA and the USSR on the number of long and medium-range nuclear missiles each side would have.

Gorbachev's shock offer on nukes ban

by MICHAEL TONER
Political Editor

SOVIET leader Mikhail Gorbachev last night raised the dazzling prospect of a nuclear breakthrough in Europe, with an offer of a deal without strings on medium-range missiles.

The offer amounts to a complete about-face on Soviet insistence that any deal on European missiles had to depend on the Americans giving up Star Wars.

If Mr Gorbachev is to be taken at his word, the road is now open for an agreement which would remove all Cruise missiles from Britain and end the threat posed by nuclear weapons in Europe.

The move reported by the Soviet news agency Tass, means Mrs Thatcher's trip to Moscow at the end of the month assumes vital importance for the whole of the Western Alliance.

There is no doubt that the Prime Minister, like every other leader in Europe, would jump at the chance to get rid of weapons which now threaten every major city on both sides of the Iron Curtain.

Deal

The deal—if it stands up to examination — would allow Britain and Italy to send Cruise missiles back to America, and the Germans to get rid of both Cruise and Pershing rockets.

The Russians, in return, would scrap their SS-20s and the older, liquid-fuelled rockets like the SS-4s.

Mr Gorbachev's offer is nothing short of sensational. The Russians have been insisting to the dismay of all European members of NATO, that a deal on medium-range missiles was not on while President Reagan was pursuing his

Star Wars dream.

All that has apparently changed.

The new Soviet proposal was being put to the United States at the current arms control talks in Geneva, Mr Gorbachev said.

"We were assured more than once that if the Soviet Union singles out the issue of medium-range missiles from the Reykjavik package, there would be no difficulty in agreeing to their elimination in Europe," he declared.

"A good opportunity is now being offered to prove that in · practice. This is being awaited by the Europeans and by other continents."

The Soviet Union, said [the two leaders] might reach agreement on substantially limiting and then abolishing the mighty strategic nuclear weapons held by the two superpowers.

That side of an arms deal, he insists, must depend on the Americans giving up their Star Wars plans.

But the issue of the "Euro-missiles" could be decided well in advance of any such overall deal.

"As far as other theatre missiles* are concerned we are ready to begin talks immediately with a view to reducing and fully eliminating them," he said.

Pressure

There is little doubt that the offer from Moscow is the best news Western governments have had since the confusion of Reykjavik.

The dramatic change in the Kremlin's position may well have been motivated by a desire to break the log-jam at the Geneva arms talks.

(From *The Sunday Express*, Sunday 1st March 1987). **Source A**

*Theatre missiles are those that can only be used in Europe. They are not powerful enough to reach the USA or USSR.

---

2 a Summarise the main proposals on nuclear weapons that Mr Gorbachev put forward, as shown in the newspaper report from the Sunday Express.

  b If NATO agrees to Gorbachev's proposals, do you think this will make a nuclear war less likely? Explain your answer.

---

3 Look at the photographs below.
  a What do these photographs show?
  b What good, if any, do you think meetings like these actually do? What are they supposed to achieve?

Source B *(top) Khrushchev and Eisenhower in the USA, 1959.* **Source C** *(centre) Nixon on arrival in China, 1979.* **Source D** *(below) Reagan and Gorbachev in Geneva, 1985*

21   Hope for the future

Source A   *Reagan and Gorbachev at Reykjavik, 1986*

You have read much in this book about the possibilities of peace if relations between the superpowers go well and the possible consequences of war if the relations turn sour. Which way will things go and how can ordinary people influence what will happen in any case?

You have seen in Chapter 20 that there have been some fruitful negotiations about arms control between the superpowers. This is a good sign of course. The photograph on this page shows President Reagan of the USA and President Gorbachev of the USSR in Reykjavik, the capital of Iceland, in October 1986. They met there for a weekend conference and, although they did not reach an agreement about arms control, they did extend the length of their talks by several hours and both sides have since said that they were very close to agreeing on a reduction in the number of nuclear weapons in Europe. Both leaders have expressed their desire to keep working towards an agreement.

---

1   *Historical Consequences*
    Many of us have played the game 'Consequences' where someone writes a man's name on a piece of paper, folds it over and passes it to the next person who writes a girl's name and so on. Historical Consequences is a similar game but it helps you to understand how events can have different results or consequences depending on who writes them down or how optimistic you are. Your teacher will divide you into groups of four or five. He or she will give the first person a piece of paper with an event that might occur involving the superpowers. (The list of suggested events are on page ii but don't spoil the fun by peeping to see what they are.) The first person in the group must write down what they think the immediate consequences of the event will be and then fold over the paper so that the next person can see only what *they* have written and not what came before. The process is repeated until everyone in the group has written something. The teacher will then summarise the events on the board. When this has been done see if you can answer the following questions.

a   Were the end consequences good ones or bad ones on the whole?
b   What does your answer to question a show about your class? Are they generally optimistic or pessimistic?
c   What difference do you think it makes if leaders enter talks optimistically (looking on the bright side) or pessimistically (looking on the dark side)?

The United Nations Organisation

One major way that the world powers have tried to maintain peace since the Second World War is through the United Nations Organisation. If you look back to Chapter 1 you will see that this organisation is divided into the Security Council made up of 15 major countries and the General Assembly which now contains 149 countries. The General Assembly needs a two-thirds majority to recommend things to the Security Council and any one of the big five on the Security Council (Britain, France, China, the USA and the USSR) can use their veto, which means that if they do not want an action to be taken by the UN then they can prevent it happening. The United Nations has in many ways been a very successful organisation. But there is always much talk about ways of improving it to make it a more effective peace-keeping organisation.

2 Work in groups again to produce a poster for a peace-keeping organisation. You must discuss the following things before including them on a poster.

1 The name of your organisation.
2 Which countries will be members? What will happen to those who refuse to join?
3 How will decisions be made? Will each country have the same number of votes and what majority will be needed to reach a decision?
4 What will be the aims of your organisation? How will you try to achieve them and what measures or actions will you take against countries who break the rules.

How can ordinary people like us do anything to help?

The picture on this page shows the Live Aid concert which took place in 1985. Entertainers from all over the world got together on one day and performed to raise money to help the starving people of Ethiopia. The event raised over 400 million pounds. It showed that people throughout the world *could* be united and work together for one cause. It is perhaps by joining organisations that hold similar views to your own that you can best influence decisions that are taken. If you are not politically minded then another way to increase understanding between peoples of the world is to write to people in other countries. The Russian and Chinese embassies in London are always pleased to try to put young people in touch with penfriends, and exchanging views about your way of life with someone from another country is a very interesting experience.

Source B *The Live Aid Concert, 1985*